Laura Dowling

WREATHS

WITH HOW-TO TUTORIALS

Laura Dowling

WREATHS

WITH HOW-TO TUTORIALS

stichting
kunstboek

This book is dedicated to B.,
connoisseur, raconteur
and Renaissance man...

Who makes me smile
every day.

CONTENTS

"Symbolizing eternal hope,
the wreath goes 'round and 'round
and where it starts or ends
cannot be found.
Woven of things that grow –
for life, and hung for holiday delight."

Throughout the world and across the chasm of time, wreaths are universal and iconic symbols of joy and celebration, of touching tributes of remembrance, and make dramatic statements of personal style.

Of all the floral art forms in the language of flowers, the wreath is arguably the most powerfully symbolic. With no beginning and no end to its circular form, the wreath represents eternity and immortality–and, according to some, is the ultimate symbol of achievement and success. In ancient Rome, a circlet of greenery on a door signified a victory in battle, honoring conquering heroes. When worn as a crown in Roman times, a wreath of leaves, greenery, small fruits and flowers conveyed occupation and social status–a highly visible depiction of academic and professional achievements. To this day, Olympic athletes traditionally don laurel wreath crowns to commemorate victory while hoisting bouquets of flowers in the air.

In Colonial Williamsburg, the ubiquitous pineapple motif brings additional meaning to traditional fruit and flower decorations, where it often appears as a medallion on wreaths and over-the-door displays. A pineapple functioned as a symbol wealth, power and friendship in the 18th century and a wreath made of pineapples continues to exude warmth and hospitality today. In Germany, four candles are placed atop fir wreaths during the Advent season, when one is lit each Sunday leading up to Christmas. During Mexican fiestas and the "El Dia de los Muertos" celebration, where departed loved ones are honored with special tributes, elaborate floral wreaths in exuberant colors with butterfly symbolism are always an essential component. I love the wreath for its elegant and timeless appeal across many different cultures and for its potential to tell a story, create a sense of place and establish compelling traditions and emotional connections.

At the White House, I created wreaths for holiday decor, to commemorate presidential birthdays, and to honor fallen heroes – including the large patriotic red, white and blue wreath the President lays at Arlington Cemetery at the Tomb of the Unknown Soldier each Memorial Day. In my White House work, I saw how the simple wreath form conveyed tradition, meaning and metaphor, representing so much more than a simple decorative placement. At home in Virginia, I use wreaths indoors and outdoors throughout the year – during the holidays, to usher in a new season, or just for pure delight and artistic expression. For me, they present an exciting art form with endless possibility for exploring creativity and innovation in design. And they are always a source of conversation in my Old Town Alexandria neighborhood.

But despite its storied tradition and symbolic significance, the wreath is in need of a major overhaul and upgrade. Perhaps hindered by ultra-practical concerns about longevity and durability that eclipse aesthetic aspirations, commercial wreaths often seem bland and boring, derivative and unimaginative, tacky and ho-hum rather than inspiring. Many of these wreaths are rendered in unattractive faux materials, clashing colors, and fashioned in somewhat dated, pedestrian designs. Too often, we have been content with less-than-stellar offerings, accepting the status quo.

The key is to expand wreath design beyond the predictable by using unexpected materials, fresh combinations and modern color palettes. Next, it's important to change expectations for how the wreath is displayed and used. Instead of placing one evergreen wreath on the door for the entire holiday season, for example, why not consider using a wreath of unusual wintry materials – purple potatoes and nandina – for the first half of the season and then switching it up with a bright red apple design? Wreaths are fun and festive – the jewelry on a house – and should be used in the spirit of celebration and symbolic expression to achieve maximum potential and effect.

This book on wreaths launches my new design series on floral art technique and inspiration – a collection of how-to books on floral design in specific areas where there is an opportunity to present fresh new ideas for wreaths, bouquets, table settings, containers and colors. Wreaths – with their special symbolism and infinite design possibility – are especially close to my heart. My sincere hope is that you will be as inspired as I am by this classic form and enjoy finding new ways to create personal statements of creativity and original seasonal, decorative floral art during the holidays and throughout the year.

"I think it's time to reinvent the wreath as a decorative and symbolic element, make it striking again, and elevate it from blasé to having *je ne sais quoi* and chic cachet."

A few thoughts. Making a wreath is a lot like telling a story with a beginning, a middle and an end. It requires a compelling plot (theme), a mix of interesting characters (design elements) and a strong narrative (technique) that builds up with a crescendo and flourish to a dramatic ending (finishing touches). In musical parlance, wreath-making is comparable to playing a jazz riff with an improvised melody and syncopated rhythms, harmonies and grace notes. Architects and engineers can relate to the process of drawing building plans, constructing a foundation, and designing a structure completed with beautiful materials. From an artistic angle, wreath design is like creating a masterpiece: mapping out lines and shapes, mixing colors, and then painting an inspiring design. In sum, making a wreath is similar to crafting every other art form – it requires a methodical thought process, technical skills and a large dose of creative inspiration.

| GETTING STARTED

Although it might seem counterintuitive for a creative project, the starting point for wreaths is actually technical and logistical – just like a pilot going over a pre-flight checklist. First, **determine the purpose and occasion** for the wreath (e.g., a holiday design, a spring fete, a wedding, birthday celebration, etc.), including **how long the wreath needs to last**. Next, **identify the context or setting** – e.g., the size and mechanics required, whether it is an indoor or outdoor wreath and if it's to be placed in a formal or informal setting. Finally, think about **how much time and effort** is required to make the wreath, including what happens to the wreath afterwards (e.g., whether fresh elements are composted or thrown away, dry elements preserved, or the wreath form saved to be used again). These considerations will determine the level of difficulty and complexity of the wreath – as well as guide overall design and style parameters.

DESIGN PROCESS

The secret of wreath-making is to create the design in levels and layers to achieve an intricate, polished and professional look. Start with a base layer to provide structure and color, followed by a layer of fruit, flowers or vegetables, and then add another level of smaller, accent pieces completed with final, finishing touches. In general, wreath-making follows the principles of design with the goal of achieving balance and harmony by utilizing color, proportion and line. When it comes to color, I tend to gravitate towards monochromatic schemes, working in a tight palette and building up textures in a focused range of a similar hue. This creates the most impact as well as a more refined and cohesive look. I think it's important to incorporate depth in the design, layering in dimension with flowing lines and escaping elements. A border of ivy (or berries, ribbon or branches woven into garlands) always adds definition to the wreath. Finally, think of where you'll be displaying your wreath and coordinate the colors, size and style to complement this backdrop.

TOOLS

A basic wreath tool kit is comprised of a few simple tools: clippers, wire cutters, scissors and various wires: paddle wire, straight wire, bark wire, and bullion wire. Over time, as you gain experience and momentum, expand your tool kit to include a variety of additional tools and elements -- wood picks, pins, water tubes, hot glue, pipe cleaners, ribbons, raffia, wool, etc. – a variety of crafting implements for creating unique and original pieces.

THE FORM

In its most basic iteration, a wreath can be hand-made from rambling branches and tumbling vines bound together to form a circle – a simple ring that is naturally elegant. For more elaborate designs requiring strength and support, choose wreath forms with a stronger, wider girth – e.g., grapevine, straw, or wire--ready-made frames you can find at the craft store. For fresh flower designs, use a floral foam wreath or foam garlands wired to a straw or grapevine frame so that the blooms have a water source. In addition to the classic circular, round form, wreath frames come in square, oval and diamond shapes, allowing for maximum flexibility in achieving your creative vision.

MATERIALS

Once you select a theme, choose design elements that will convey the story from start to finish. For a fresh look, think outside the typical, traditional wreath recipe and expand the boundaries to blend fresh and faux, dried and non-floral materials, with an unexpected mix of fruit, flowers and vegetables leading the way. I like to use new combinations such as potatoes and orchids in surprising color combinations. In general, use a variety of elements focusing on color and texture: dried grasses, gathered pinecones, collected shells, fabricated ribbons and on and on – mixing and matching these materials to achieve the desired effect and overall vision. The key is to incorporate multiple sizes, shapes and forms (e.g., round, pointy, and delicate fruits or flowers) that have different finishes (e.g., shiny, matte or natural) and bold color combinations (purple and red, plum and lime green, etc.). By expanding the range of elements used in these designs, it's possible to create completely new concepts – a new art form: wreaths that make a statement and can be used for many occasions throughout the year. Although I often start with a concept and outline of a plan, I leave room to improvise as I go along – this is the space where creativity ensues.

THEMES AND CONCEPTS

An overarching theme or concept is an integral part of wreath design, influencing the choice of materials and colors and setting the overall mood or tone. A successful theme can be inspired by a place (e.g., Provence or the north woods), a nostalgic memory (e.g., grandmother's apple pie), a color (Bordeaux wine), a scent (honeysuckle vine), a texture (blue velvet), etc. The possibilities are truly endless.

In general, I've used a few basic techniques throughout the book, replicated in many of the designs: a sturdy loop for hanging, base layer, wired elements, accent garlands and finishing touches. My starting point is always the foundation, including focal point or main materials (usually the largest fruit or flowers), accent elements (smaller items and more delicate textures), followed by the finishing touches—the lightest elements that float in and above the wreath. Here are the basic techniques to master as you launch your wreath-making adventures.

TECHNIQUES

THE BASE LAYER

The base layer is the foundation of the wreath that can be made from a variety of materials: evergreens, folded leaves, burlap, ribbons and paper. Much like a mat that goes underneath an area rug, the base layer creates a textured backdrop for lifting and supporting the materials on the wreath, preventing them from slipping. In this case, the base layer also adds color, complementing the design and coordinating with the fruit, vegetable and flower elements. Here are my favorite techniques for creating the base layer.

RUCHED RIBBON GARLAND

This technique is a fundamental key to the overall look – not only does it provide dynamic color and texture, it is perhaps the best method for supporting the materials and framing the wreath. The ruched ribbon is basically a one-sided ribbon garland that results in textured loops. It can be made from various widths and finishes (e.g., satin, burlap, etc.) and can be re-used again and again. For the festive and wintry reindeer wreath pictured at left, I used faux fur ribbon as the backdrop for the silver bauble and acorn design. Here's how to create the ruched ribbon garland:

WHAT *you'll need*
1 ½ - 3 inch ribbon (e.g., satin, burlap, mesh, etc.).
Bullion wire
Scissors
Wire cutters
Wreath form

HOW-TO *instructions*

1. Holding the bullion wire in one hand, create a 1-inch loop with the other.
2. Wrap the bullion wire tightly around the base of the loop as close to the base as possible.
3. Wrap the wire around the loop, going around twice or 3 times.
4. Holding the loop with the ribbon extending behind it, make another loop as close to the original loop as possible. Wrap the bullion wire around tightly to secure.
5. Continue making a garland of loops in this manner until there is enough material to cover the top and sides of the wreath.
6. Add the ruched ribbon to the wreath frame, tying the sides with bullion wire, working around the wreath until the form is covered.

EVERGREENS AND FOLIAGE

For a natural effect, use sprigs of evergreens, ivy or lemon leaves to create an organic base layer. The technique involves bundling greens with the bullion wire, and laying them across the wreath in rows, using the paddle wire to bind them to the form. Here are the step by step techniques for a simple evergreen design:

WHAT *you'll need*

Evergreen branches
Bullion wire
Green paddle wire
Clippers
Wire cutters

HOW-TO *instructions*

1. Using the bullion wire, bind 3 – 4 sprigs of greens at the base, creating a bundle.
2. Continue creating bundles in this manner, checking to make sure that they are all the same size.
3. Working in rows from left to right across the wreath, lay the bundles across the sides and top of the wreath, wrapping with paddle wire around the wreath.
4. Holding the paddle wire, continue adding rows of evergreen bundles, over-lapping the next row so that it covers the bullion wire, covering the entire wreath.
5. Wrap the paddle wire around to the back, tying off the end.

TIP

Work evenly and precisely for best effect. If done correctly, the underside of the garland will resemble a textured pattern.

TIP

Keep the evergreen bundles small and precise for a neat, professional look. For a more rustic version, cut longer lengths of the evergreen stems, allowing them to flow naturally around the wreath.

FOLDED AND STAPLED LEAVES

Wreaths made of simple green leaves are a striking and elegant option throughout the year; they look especially good on a red or white door. When leaves are folded and pleated, the technique creates an interesting, organic texture with a couture effect. Use the folded leaf wreath on its own or as a base material for fruit, flower and vegetable designs. These wreaths work well in a variety of settings, evoking either a classical or modern vibe depending upon where they're displayed. Here are ideas for using folded and stapled aspidistra leaves – as a traditional wreath or a basis for more elaborate designs.

WHAT *you'll need*

Several bunches of aspidistra leaves
Scissors
Bullion wire
6-inch wired wood picks
Wire cutters
Grapevine wreath

HOW-TO *instructions*

1 Cut the leaf starting at the base, following the shape all the way around to the other side.
2 Fold the center piece over to create a loop.
3 Take the end and weave it in and around the loop, creating a ribbon-like effect.
4 Tie the end to the base with bullion wire, clipping the stem down to leave two-inches.
5 Wire the "ribbon" aspidistra to the wood picks.
6 Working left to right across the wreath in rows, insert the stems into the grapevine form until the entire surface is covered.

VARIATIONS

Fold the aspidistra leaves in half to create a ribbon-like loop; staple at the base. Insert the folded leaves into the grapevine form, covering the entire wreath. Or, fold lemon leaves in half, light side facing out, stapling close to the fold. Working left to right in rows across the wreath, pin the leaves to a straw wreath form, creating a scalloped, fish-scale effect.

TIP

Aspidistra and lemon leaves (salal) are excellent choices for wreath designs since they are long-lasting and dry well in place.

GARLAND BASE LAYER

Another wreath-making technique that can be used by itself or as a base layer involves creating narrow garlands that are then wired to the form. The technique involves wrapping small bundles of leaves or foliage to a bind wire, creating a garland and then attaching it to the top of the frame. Here, I've used fresh magnolia leaves on a grapevine form, finished with a light touch of silver paint.

WHAT *you'll need*
2 bunches of magnolia leaves
Bullion wire
Bind wire
Paddle wire
Straw wreath form
Clippers
Wire cutters

HOW-TO *instructions*

1 Cut the magnolia into 4-inch pieces, bundling 3 stems together at the base with the bullion wire, creating multiple bundles.
2 Cut a length of bind wire a few inches longer than the circumference of the wreath.
3 Using the paddle wire, wrap the magnolia bundles around the bind wire, overlapping each layer of leaves to disguise the bullion wire, securing the bundles tightly at the base, leaving a few inches of bind wire on each end.
4 Continue adding and wrapping the magnolia bundles, creating a garland.
5 Tie the garland to the top of the wreath form, securing it with the paddle wire to the frame.

TULLE AND ORGANZA

Another effective (and quick) method for creating a base layer is to wrap the wreath form with tulle or organza sheets that are readily available at craft and floral supply stores. The relatively stiff fabric comes in a variety of colors, providing bulk and texture for a variety of themes and designs. For holiday versions, tuck in strands of LED lights to provide a luminous glow like in the "Sweet Dreams" wreath pictured on the right.

WHAT *you'll need*
1 – 2 organza sheets
Grapevine wreath
Bullion wire

HOW-TO *instructions*

1 Hold a corner of the organza sheet and tuck it into the side of the wreath.

2 Wrap the organza loosely around the wreath, keeping the width consistent all the way around.

3 Secure the end by tucking it into the grapevine frame, tying it with bullion wire.

PAPER

Paper is a versatile (and cost-effective) choice for a base layer with myriad applications. I often use plain white paper folded into textured pieces as a backdrop for wintry designs; the folded "honeycomb" design was the basis for my "Queen Bee" wreath. For the bee design, I used grocery bags that were cut, folded and gilded into 3-dimensional pieces and then glued onto the frame. Wrapping paper – with its infinite array of colors and patterns – is another great material. Here are a couple of techniques for working with paper to create textured base layers for themed wreath designs.

WHAT *you'll need*

Paper (e.g., craft paper, white paper, etc.)
Scissors
6-inch wired wood picks
Grapevine wreath
Hot glue gun
Hot glue
24 karat gold craft spray paint

HOW-TO *instructions*

1 Cut white paper into 3-inch squares, pinch the middle and wire to the wood picks, creating a floret.
2 Insert the florets into the grapevine form, working back and forth in rows across the wreath until the entire surface is covered.

HONEYCOMB VARIATION

1 Cut brown craft paper (or grocery store bags) into squares.
2 Fold into geometric shaped "paper catchers" to resemble a honeycomb motif.
3 Spray the "paper catchers" with gold spray paint.
4 Using the hot glue gun, apply the paper catchers to the wreath, covering the sides and top all the way around the frame.

WIRING MATERIALS

THE MAIN LAYER

The secret to a professional looking wreath lies in the use of straight florist wire to build the composition in even horizontal rows. In general, use the thinnest wire possible that will hold the fruit or vegetables. The 18-inch 24-gauge straight wire works best for this purpose. Sometimes, when incorporating large or heavy materials, such as pumpkins or cabbages, you'll need a heavier gauge wire like 18-inch 20-gauge wire. You can find straight wire at the floral supply store. Here is the technique for wiring fruit and vegetables to a wreath form:

HOW-TO *instructions*

1 Pierce the fruit or vegetable with the straight wire, stringing several together to create a garland. Note: the number will vary according to the size of the fruit/vegetable.

2 Lay the garland across the wreath form so that the fruit/vegetables cover the sides and top of the wreath, wrap the wire ends to the back, twisting to secure. Clip the excess wire.

3 Working in rows around the wreath, continue adding garlands of fruit or vegetables until the entire wreath is covered.

WIRING MATERIALS

THE ACCENT LAYER

After the base layer is complete, the next step is to add a layer of accent materials, typically smaller fruits and vegetables that float in and around the elements. One technique involves wiring accent elements to wired wood picks like the pine cones pictured at right. Additional accent elements can be flowers, leaves, berries and a broad range of non-floral material, too (e.g., marshmallows, balloons, etc.). The technique involves creating garlands by stringing the accent material on bullion wire and placing it over the top of the base layer. Here is the technique for wiring an accent layer of fruit (or other accent materials):

WHAT *you'll need*
Small fruits or vegetables
Straight wire
Bullion wire
6-inch wired wood picks

HOW-TO *instructions*

1 String small fruit or berries onto a straight wire (thinner gauge).

2 Lay the garland across the wreath, wrapping the ends to the back and twisting together to secure. Clip the excess wire.

3 Working in rows around the wreath, continue adding layers of accent fruit material until it is evenly spaced around the wreath.

4 Continue filling in the wreath with bundles of small fruits or berries wired to the wood picks.

TIP

Wire two pieces of straight wire together for extra length, creating extra height and dimension in the accent layer.

HANGING AND DISPLAYING THE WREATH

In general, wreaths are works of floral art that are meant to be displayed vertically, hung in a window or on a gate or door. This requires a strategic method of hanging – a solid mechanic to ensure that the wreath stays in place rather than tumbles to the ground. Wreaths are also effective as table and window displays. I typically use barked wire – a heavy wire with a natural fiber covering to create a loop for hanging wreaths. It can slip over a nail, be wrapped with ribbon or additional decorative cording. Here's how to create a loop for hanging that will support heavy fruits and vegetables – and a wide variety of other designs:

WHAT *you'll need*
Bark wire
Wreath form
Wire cutters

HOW-TO *instructions*
1 Cut a long 18-inch length of bark wire.
2 Wrap the bark wire around the wreath, doubling it, to create a 3-inch loop.
3 Twist the bark wire at the top of the wreath to secure it.

FINISHING TOUCHES

The final layer is actually the most visible, leading the eye into the design. It involves adding finishing touches – flowers, berries, greenery, vines -- that float in and around the wreath to create texture, dimension and interest. To achieve the additional height and width that extends beyond the actual frame, use a few additional tools (water picks, wired wood picks and pipe cleaners) to create "butterflies" with orchids, gloriosa lilies, and delicate greenery. Pipe cleaners and paper-covered wire can be woven into borders that support grasses, vines and other materials, bringing lightness to the design. Wrap pipe cleaners in wool to add color, creating a vine-like effect. Here are a few techniques for creating inspiring finishing touches:

BUTTERFLY ORCHIDS

I often use orchid blossoms in my wreaths; the petal shape resembles a butterfly, and when several are placed in the design, they add a colorful, whimsical touch.

WHAT *you'll need*
Orchid stems (mokara, phalaeonopsis, dendrobium, cattleya, etc.)
4-inch water picks

HOW-TO *instructions*
1 Cut individual orchid blossoms (or small pieces of orchids with multiple blooms) and insert into the water picks.
2 Place the orchids so that they float in and around the wreath, including the interior and outside edges.

VARIATION: *Delicate garlands*
Tie snippets of leaves, rosebuds or berries together with bullion wire, creating garlands that can be woven in and around the wreath.

VARIATION: *Pipe cleaner border*
Create a pipe cleaner border by linking pipe cleaners end to end and then wrapping with twine or wool to create additional texture. Attach the border to the exterior edge of the wreath with bullion wire. Use this structure to weave in additional greens, vines and flowers.

TIP
Wrap the water pick with lemon leaves to disguise the plastic; tie it with bullion wire to secure the greenery.

| ADDITIONAL THOUGHTS

An environmental approach. As a former policy analyst and communications strategist for The Nature Conservancy, I always approach floral design from an eco-friendly and sustainable practices perspective. I think it makes good sense to work with materials that are sustainably harvested, re-usable and recyclable and ultimately have a low-impact on the environment. And it's heartening to see that floral suppliers are following suit and creating tools and materials that are bio-degradable, re-usable and compostable – a trend that is sure to gain momentum going forward. When it comes to floral artistry and design – like many areas in life – moderation and balance are key: do what you can, do what makes sense and make informed everyday choices to help have a positive impact on the environment. Most of the wreath designs in this book can be re-purposed, re-invented and re-designed after the fresh materials fade – and are made in the spirit of this pragmatic, environmentally-friendly approach.

A NOTE ABOUT CLIMATE AND NATURE

After years of trials and tribulations (and more than a few humorous run-ins with neighborhood squirrels and birds), I've learned to take a pre-emptive, proactive approach when placing wreaths outdoors. A light spray of hot pepper sauce or acrylic floor wax will keep unwanted critters at bay while adding a protective sheen. In general, if you live in an area with temperature extremes and/or that is prone to various wildlife, you'll want to stay away from delicate, fresh materials – and instead use faux, dried and non-floral options on your exterior door. Most of the fresh fruit and vegetable designs in this book can be rendered in a range of suitable substitute faux and non-floral materials. Some ideas, especially potato or succulent wreaths, are durable and long-lasting and can be used almost anywhere throughout the year. In general, I see my wreath designs as special occasion floral art with an expiration date – and an exciting opportunity to create new and innovative replacements. If you approach wreath-making with the goal of surprising and delighting viewers with inspired designs (tempered by practical realities) – your wreaths will be an aesthetic success – and survive the elements.

A NOTE ABOUT MATERIALS

Necessity is often the mother of invention -- and design. I started using fruits and vegetables in my wreaths when I noticed that they were hardier and more available than flowers – especially during the winter months. When working with edible materials, I think it's important to consider using them for this purpose once their decorative objective is complete. In this case, working with wooden skewers and tooth picks (rather than wire) will allow you to pivot quickly from the design table to the kitchen table – where many of the wreaths can be turned into soups, salads and other delectable treats – while others (like dried flowers and citrus fruits) can be made into potpourri and additional decorations. If a gourmet meal or scented sachet is not in the cards, you can still create value by sending the used material to the compost heap – or, in the case of apples, to your friendly neighborhood horse farm.

A NOTE ABOUT THE BOOK

For me, creativity boils down to inspiration – that intangible spark that leads to new ideas, originality and innovation in design. While many floristry books are organized by color or by season, my goal is to focus on the actual well-spring of inspiration – the natural places and landscapes that provide a theme, provoke a memory, and create a strong sense of emotion. I think this is the most compelling source of creativity in floristry. Each chapter is designed to create context and background for my favorite wreath creations, evoking a sense of time and place, journeys to exotic locales, nostalgic memories of home, and celebrations of nature's bounty. There are designs inspired by the garden, the sea, the harvest, woodland forests, wildflower fields and meadows – and even by elusive and beautiful dreams. Finally, I've included notes about level of difficulty and projected longevity for each wreath design. I hope you will enjoy my stories and designs, and, from the examples and how to instructions contained in these pages, find new ways to celebrate life's key moments -- re-inventing the classic, symbolic and inspiring wreath motif in your own personal style.

| THE WREATHS

WHAT *you'll need*

TOOLS: Bark wire
1 can of silver spray craft paint
Silver bullion wire
Straight wire (thinner gauge)
Clippers
Wire cutters
Scissors
6-inch wired wood picks

MATERIALS:
1 18-inch grapevine wreath
5 bags of medium size marshmallows
1 roll of silver wrapping paper
1 bunch of white branches
1 bunch of silver ruscus
1 bag of white pipe cleaners
1 bag of white feathers (from the craft store)
1 bunch of silver eucalyptus pods
A small amount of natural white wool
Berried ivy

Inspired by the classic Tchaikovsky ballet, this "Swan Lake" wreath is a woodland fantasy of wintry elements that evoke the exquisite fairy tale of a midnight dance across a shimmering moonlit lake: marshmallow clouds, frosted branches with gilded leaves and ethereal white feather garlands. The silver ruscus and sparkly wrapping paper add subtle sparkle to the design, while the mix of creamy white textures and branches seem to dance and twirl around the form.

SWAN LAKE

HOW-TO *instructions*

1 Wrap the bark wire around the wreath to create a loop for hanging.

2 Spray the grapevine wreath with the silver paint.

3 Cut the silver paper into a small square, gather in the middle and bind with the bullion wire, creating a floret.

4 Attach the paper florets to wood picks and insert in the wreath to create a light base layer.

5 Using the straight wire, string 7 marshmallows together to create a garland and place it across the front of the wreath. Tie the ends of the wire behind the wreath to secure the garland.

6 Cut the eucalyptus pods into 4-inch pieces and wire them to the wood picks. Insert them in and around the wreath to add a layer of texture.

7 Cut pieces of silver eucalyptus and wire them to the wood picks. Insert them throughout the wreath, including the inside and outside edges.

8 Cut 6-inch pieces of white branches and wire them to the wood picks. Add them to the wreath, focusing on the perimeter.

9 Weave white pipe cleaners to the outside edge of the grapevine wreath, twisting them to form a crisscross pattern, resembling a snowflake. Wrap the white wool around the pipe cleaners.

10 Cut the ivy berries into small bunches and wire them to the wood picks. Add them into the wreath as an accent touch.

11 Using the bullion wire, wrap the ends of the feathers to create a garland, leaving about 4 – 5-inch in between. Wrap the feather garlands around the wreath as a finishing touch.

In the untamed wilderness of Oregon and Washington's Cascade Mountain range, majestic evergreen trees dominate the landscape with their impressive profile and stature, often towering 130 feet above the forest floor. My favorite trees are the Noble and Douglas firs: their emerald green branches, fresh, citrusy scent and lush canopy create iconic beauty – as well as a lush habitat for woodland creatures large and small: elk, mule deer, mountain goats, bighorn sheep, black bears and mountain lions. I often use fresh evergreens for holiday wreaths or as a base for fruit, flower and vegetable designs. The greens form a cushion and support the wreath materials; the evergreen tips are fragrant and long-lasting, holding up throughout the season. In its elegant simplicity, the evergreen wreath stands alone as a classic, seasonal motif, making a statement with or without additional adornment and/or a jaunty bow as a finishing touch.

WHAT *you'll need*

TOOLS: 18-inch straw wreath form
Bark wire
Bullion wire
Paddle wire
Clippers
Wire cutters
6-inch wired wood picks

MATERIALS:
3 bunches of evergreen fir tips
(e.g., pine, noble fir, cedar, juniper, etc.)
1 bunch of privet or ivy berries
1 bag of small pinecones
Ribbon trim (optional)

DESIGN *note*

Cut the bundles in even lengths and apply them uniformly in horizontal rows across the wreath to create a polished, professional finish. Add a classic red, green or gold bow for a festive holiday touch.

| EVERGREEN FIR

HOW-TO *instructions*

1 Wrap the bark wire around the wreath frame to create a loop for hanging.
2 Cut the fir tips into 4-inch pieces, bundling 4 – 5 pieces together, tying each bundle securely at the base with bullion wire.
3 Working left to right, lay individual bundles across the wreath form, wrapping the paddle wire around the base of the bundles, holding the paddle wire in one continuous piece.
4 Continue adding rows of evergreen bundles, layering them an-inch above the base of the previous row to hide the wires.
5 Working in even rows, continue layering and wrapping bundles until the wreath is covered.
6 Using the wood picks, wire pieces of privet or ivy berries and insert them in and around the wreath.
7 Add small pinecones in the same manner.
8 As an optional finishing touch, add a festive ribbon bow.

The humble pinecone – a simple gift of nature during the autumn and winter seasons – is one of the most versatile materials for crafting unique wreaths and seasonal displays. The pinecone's spiraling form and earthy brown color lend it to a variety of treatments and styles from classic simplicity to whimsical, contemporary designs. For this iteration of a pinecone wreath, I added bright fuchsia wool and ribbons for a fanciful effect.

WHAT *you'll need*

TOOLS: Bark wire
Bullion wire
6-inch wired wood picks
Clippers
Wire cutters
Scissors

MATERIALS:
1 18-inch pinecone wreath
1 roll of 3-inch fuchsia ribbon
1 skein of thick fuchsia wool
1 skein of thick red wool
25 red crabapples

| PINECONES, WOOL & CRABAPPLES

HOW-TO *instructions*

1 Cut 6-inches of ribbon into a continuous piece, wrapping and tying to create a curly form. Secure with bullion wire.

2 Continue creating enough curly forms with the ribbon to encircle the entire wreath.

3 Using the paddle wire, bind the forms together, creating several garlands.

4 Attach the ribbon garlands to the outside edge of the wreath by wiring the ends to wood picks and inserting into the grapevine frame.

5 Cut the wool into 2-inch pieces and wire on to the wood picks, leaving a few inches between the wood and the wool.

6 Insert the wool picks into the frame so that the entire wreath is covered – positioning the wool so that it floats above the wreath.

7 Wire crabapples to the wood picks and insert them throughout the wreath.

DESIGN *note*

Use either a purchased pinecone wreath or make one from scratch using the directions on p. 30.

TIP

Use gold paddle wire for the best effect.

As a child growing up in Washington state, I remember going on annual autumn excursions in the foothills of the Cascade Mountains, a place of lush wildflower meadows and enchanted pine forests. One of my key objectives was to gather pinecones of various shapes and sizes from the moss-covered forest floor to use in holiday crafting projects: wreaths and mantel garlands as well as orange and cinnamon-scented potpourri. At the White House, pinecones became one of my favorite floral art crafting materials that were used in many projects including detailed columns rendered in a 3-dimensional cube motif. For this wreath, I used a mix of gilded pinecones in various sizes and magnolia pods wired to a grapevine base. The gold paint and simple, clean lines create a classically elegant seasonal display.

GILDED PINECONES

WHAT *you'll need*

TOOLS: Bark wire
Paddle wire
Straight wire
Clippers
Wire cutters
6-inch wired wood picks

MATERIALS:
1 18-inch grape vine wreath frame
8 bags of cinnamon scented pinecones from the craft store (or an equivalent amount from the woods)
24 karat gold craft spray paint
12 magnolia pods

HOW-TO *instructions*

1 Wrap the bark wire around the frame to create a loop for hanging.
2 Spray the pinecones and magnolia pods with a light layer of gold spray paint, covering all sides.
3 Using the paddle wire, create garlands of 3 pinecones by wrapping individual pine cones and twisting the wire, adding a pine cone, leaving a 2 inch interval of wire in between pinecones and about 6 – 8 inches on each end.
4 Working in rows, wrap the pinecone garlands across the frame, tying the ends securely in the back. Cut the excess wire.
5 Continue adding strings of pinecones until the entire wreath is covered.
6 Wire the magnolia pods and wrap them in and around the pine cones to create additional texture.
7 As a finishing touch, attach individual pinecones to wired wood picks and insert them into the grapevine frame where needed to add fullness.
8 Bundle small pieces of variegated holly together and wire them to the wood picks.
9 Insert the variegated holly in and around the wreath as a finishing touch.

After a snowfall, the landscape sparkles and glistens with its top coat of winter white, drawing us into a magical wonderland vignette. Lyrical and enchanting, the snow-covered surroundings envelop everything in an idyllic dream set in a Currier and Ives scene. This wreath of white pinecones and berries with a snowflake border celebrates the quiet beauty and majestic splendor of the winter landscape, conjuring snow-kissed evergreens, the scent of pine and cedar, and the sheer delight of being home for the holidays.

WHITE PINECONES & SNOWBERRIES

WHAT *you'll need*

TOOLS: 1 18-inch white grapevine wreath
1 can white craft spray paint
Bark wire
Paddle wire
Bullion wire
Clippers
Wire cutters
Scissors
6-inch wired wood picks

MATERIALS:
8 bag of white pinecones or gather from the woods and spray with white paint
1 bunch of white snowberries (fresh or faux)
5 stems of mini white pine ornaments
1 bunch of white branches
1 bag of white pipe cleaners
A small amount of white natural wool

HOW-TO *instructions*

1   Wrap the bark wire around the wreath to create a loop for hanging.
2   Create garlands of 5 white pinecones by wrapping the paddle wire tightly around the pine cone and adding additional pinecones, leaving a 2-inch space in between and 6 – 8-inches of wire on each end.
3   Position the pinecone string across the top of the wreath, tying the wire securely in the back. Cut the excess wire.
4   Continue adding the pinecone strings until the entire wreath is covered.
5   Using the wood picks, wire the mini pinecones into the wreath to create an additional layer and texture.
6   Cut the snowberries into small pieces and wire them to the wood picks. Add them in and around the wreath.
7   Working on the outside edge of the wreath, insert the white pipe cleaners into the edge of the wreath, crossing them to create a snowflake border.
8   Wrap the exposed edges with natural wool as a finishing touch.

Throughout the verdant lowlands of the Southeast United States, spanning from East Texas to Florida and Georgia through the Carolinas and Virginia, the southern magnolia grandiflora tree reigns supreme as the evergreen queen. A classic symbol of dignity and nobility, the magnolia tree is prized for its shiny, long-lasting emerald green leaves with a velvety suede brown underside and gigantic white scented blooms. Unequivocally elegant and sophisticated, always stylish, magnolia leaf decorations – wreaths, swags, garlands – are equally at home in a rustic cabin or elegant mansion. Magnolia is beautiful on its own but can also be embellished with a light touch of gold or silver paint for distinctively festive holiday displays.

WHAT *you'll need*

TOOLS: Bark wire
Bullion wire
Paddle wire
Clippers
Wire cutters
Scissors

MATERIALS:
1 18-inch straw wreath
3 bunches of fresh magnolia tips
1 ½ yards of wide copper organza ribbon

TIP

Place the magnolia leaves in a mixture of glycerin and water (1 part glycerin / 2 parts water) and soak for 2-6 days to keep the pliable texture of the magnolia fresher longer.

CLASSIC MAGNOLIA

HOW-TO *instructions*

1 Wrap the bark wire around the wreath to create a loop for hanging.
2 Create tight, even bundles of magnolia leaves by binding 3 – 4 pieces of 4-inch branches together with the bullion wire.
3 Working left to right, lay 4 bundles of leaves across the top of the wreath, covering the sides and front.
4 Attach the bundles to the frame, wrapping the paddle wire tightly at the base, holding the paddle wire to wrap in one continuous piece.
5 Working in rows from left to right, continue adding bundles of magnolia leaves, overlapping the bundles and wrapping them with the paddle wire until the entire wreath is covered.
6 Cut and tie the paddle wire, securing the end around the back.
7 As a finishing touch, tie the organza ribbon in the middle of the wreath, cutting the ends in a dovetail pattern.

The woodlands style lends itself to a variety of treatments and materials, including embellishment with gold and silver paint, crystals, a dusting of "snow," and even the addition of topiary forest creatures. A red fox medallion made of red pistachios on a pinecone wreath creates a striking Virginia hunt-country theme, while a silver-brunia covered wild boar will add an unexpected element of French country charm and whimsy. Here, I've created a reindeer medallion made of pinecone scales placed atop a textured wreath of faux fur ribbon and a silvery wreath to create a festive woodlands holiday display.

WHAT *you'll need*

TOOLS:

Bark wire
Bind wire
Bullion wire
Paddle wire
6-inch wired wood picks
Glue gun
Glue sticks
Clippers
Wire cutters
Scissors

SILVER REINDEER

MATERIALS:

1 18-inch straw wreath
1 16-inch silver wreath (with acorns, leaves, pinecones and other woodlands elements)
1 papier mache reindeer head topiary form
2 bags of pinecones with large scales
1 can of silver spray paint
2 rolls of 3-inch wide mink-colored faux fur ribbon
2 bunches of silver brunia
Green trailing ivy

DESIGN *note*

Use a pre-made, silvery commercial wreath as a short-cut for this design. Or, create the silver wreath from scratch using fresh and/or faux acorns, leaves, etc.

HOW-TO *instructions*

1 Wrap the bark wire around the wreath to create a loop for hanging.
2 Using the paddle wire and faux fur ribbon, create a base layer using the ruched ribbon technique.
3 Attach the ruched fur to the straw form, covering the sides and top.
4 Place the silver wreath on the form and secure it to the base with paddle wire. Tie the wire at the top and bottom and on the left and right side.
5 Wire small pieces of silver brunia to the wood picks and insert them.
6 Using the clippers, cut pinecone scales, clipping as close to the base.
7 Hot glue the scales to the topiary form in an overlapping pattern, creating a fish-scale motif, covering the entire surface.
8 Spray the reindeer with a light coating of silver paint.
9 Using the bind wire, attach the reindeer medallion to the wreath, wrapping it tightly to secure.
10 As a finishing touch, add lengths of trailing ivy, focusing on all the borders.

Ivy has always held deep symbolic meaning, representing eternity, fidelity and friendship. In the Middle Ages, ivy took on an association with wine, signifying Bacchus, the god of wine, who is typically depicted adorned with ivy and grapes. According to legend, if a branch of ivy was hung outside a tavern, it indicated that the establishment sold wine, which was an effective means of advertising convivial libations and festive gatherings. As holiday décor, ivy hits all the right notes – creating a merry greeting, welcoming friends and family in the spirit of the season. For this evergreen wreath, I've used woodland bush ivy to create a festive study in holiday red and green.

IVY & BERRY

WHAT *you'll need*

TOOLS: Bark wire
Bullion wire
Paddle wire
4-inch wired wood picks
4-inch water picks

MATERIALS:
1 18-inch grape vine wreath
1 bunch of green bush ivy
2 bunches red berries
(e.g., Hypericum or holly berries)
1 roll of 3-inch wired edge red ribbon
(optional)

HOW-TO *instructions*

1 Wrap the wreath with bark wire to create a loop for hanging.
2 Bundle 3 – 4 pieces of 4-inch ivy, wiring them to the wood picks.
3 Working left to right in even rows across the wreath, insert the wood pick/ivy bundles into the form.
4 Continue adding ivy bundles in this manner until the entire wreath is covered.
5 Cut the red berries into small 3-inch pieces and insert in water picks.
6 Add the berries in and around the wreath to create color and texture.
7 As an optional finishing touch, add a satin ribbon bow.

In the quaint German city of Dusseldorf, situated among fairy-tale woodlands and vineyards of the North Rhine-Westphalia, autumn unfolds like a harvest feast in sparkling golden splendor. Along one of the stone and Tudor building-lined streets in the old part of town, locals and visitors alike flock to an unassuming window where they line up to taste Killepitsch – the famous liqueur unique to Dusseldorf. This potent ruby red drink, made from woodland fruits, berries, herbs and spices, is lauded for its medicinal purposes and – at 42% alcohol content -- is known for packing a powerful punch. This wreath of autumn berries, crabapples and cinnamon sticks is designed to create a similar visual impact as this famous German liqueur – without any of the potential consequences.

WHAT *you'll need*

TOOLS:
Bark wire
Straight wire (thinner gauge)
Red bullion wire
6 inch wired wood picks

BERRY SPICE

MATERIALS:

1 18-inch grapevine wreath
2 rolls of 1 ½ inch berry ribbon
3 bunches pumpkin trees
2 pounds crabapples
3 bags of fresh cranberries
2 bunches pepper berries
30 cinnamon sticks
Berried ivy

HOW-TO *instructions* | 2 W +

1   Wrap the bark wire around the wreath to create a loop for hanging.
2   Create a ribbon base layer using the ruched ribbon technique.
3   Using the straight wire, pierce the ornamental pumpkins, stringing 2 together.
4   Lay the pumpkin garland across the wreath, wrap the ends to the back, twist tightly to secure. Cut the excess wire.
5   Working in rows around the wreath, add additional pumpkin garlands in this manner, spacing them evenly.
6   Next, create crabapple garlands with the straight wire, stringing 5 together.
7   Place the crabapple garland across the wreath, wrap the ends around, secure in the back.
8   Continue adding the crabapple garlands until the entire wreath is covered.
9   Wire small pieces of pepper berry to the wood picks and insert in and around the edges, focusing on the internal and external edges.
10 Using the red bullion wire, create several cinnamon stick garlands, wrapping the wire in the middle.

When working with pinecones and other woodsy elements that are characterized by subtle, muted hues, it's often important to incorporate a colorful accent touch. For this version of the pinecone wreath, I used a mix of natural and gilded pinecones, accented with sugar snap peas and variegated holly. The green peas add a note of whimsy and freshness, while the holly exudes an appropriate seasonal sensibility.

PINECONES & SUGAR SNAP PEAS

WHAT *you'll need*

TOOLS: Bark wire
Paddle wire
Straight wire
Clippers
Wire cutters
6-inch wired wood picks

MATERIALS:

1 18-inch grape vine wreath frame
10 bags of cinnamon scented pinecones from the craft store (or an equivalent amount from the woods)
24 karat gold craft spray paint
1 ½ pounds of sugar snap peas
1 bunch of variegated holly

HOW-TO *instructions*

1 Wrap the bark wire around the frame to create a loop for hanging.
2 Spray 3 bags of pinecones with a light layer of gold paint.
3 Using the paddle wire, create garlands of 5 pinecones (mixing gold and natural together) by wrapping individual pine cones and twisting the wire, adding a pine cone, leaving a 2-inch interval of wire in between pinecones and about 6 – 8-inches on each end.
4 Working in rows, wrap the pinecone garlands across the frame, tying the ends securely in the back. Cut the excess wire.
5 Continue adding strings of pinecones until the entire wreath is covered.
6 Create small bundles of sugar snap peas using the wired wood picks, piercing 3 – 4 together and tying them so that the snap peas are about 2-inches above the wood base.
7 Insert the wired sugar snap peas into the grapevine frame so that they float above the wreath in various directions.
8 Bundle small pieces of variegated holly together and wire them to the wood picks.
9 Insert the variegated holly in and around the wreath as a finishing touch.

Natural and striking in color and form, pinecones can be painted colors, gilded or dipped in white paint to resemble snow. Try bleaching them for a trendy neutral effect or embellish with brightly hued berries and ribbons for more colorful and traditional designs. Here, I've used cranberries and magnolia pods to create a cozy wreath that reminds me of kitchen pomanders of cranberry spice and sweet cinnamon-infused mulled cider – a perfect way to spread indoor (and outdoor) holiday cheer.

| PINECONES & RED BERRIES

WHAT *you'll need*

TOOLS: Green paddle wire
Bullion wire
Clippers
Wire cutters
Scissors
Floral cold glue

MATERIALS:
1 18-inch pinecone wreath
1 roll of copper/brown 1 ½-inch ribbon
3 bags of cinnamon scented pinecones
  (or an equivalent amount from the woods)
3 pounds of cranberries
16 magnolia pods
Holly leaves

HOW-TO *instructions*

1 Wrap the burgundy ribbon around the wreath to create a loop for hanging.
2 Craft a ribbon base layer using the ruched ribbon technique.
3 Using the paddle wire, make garlands of pinecones by twisting the wire around the center, wiring 4 together, leaving 2-inches in between.
4 Lay the pinecone garland across the wreath, wrapping the ends around and securing in the back. Cut the excess wire.
5 Working in rows around the wreath, continue adding pinecones in this manner to cover the entire form.
6 Create 8 garlands of magnolia pods, wiring 2 together.
7 Place the magnolia pod garlands over the top of the wreath, positioning the pods to fit in and around the pinecones. Twist the wire ends together in back.
8 Using the bullion wire, create cranberry garlands (about 8 – 10-inches in length), leaving 6 – 8-inches of wire on each end.
9 Wrap the cranberry garlands around the wreath like ribbons, creating a variety of patterns and lines. Secure the ends in back, cut the excess wire.
10 Using the cold glue, attach individual holly leaves to create a touch of green throughout the wreath.

WHAT *you'll need*

TOOLS: Bark wire
Bullion wire
Straight wire (thinner gauge)
Clippers
Wire cutters
Scissors
4-inch water picks
6-inch wire wood picks

MATERIALS:
1 18-inch grapevine wreath
1 roll 1 ½-inch aubergine satin ribbon
Approximately 100 plums
3 pints of grape tomatoes
2 pints of black cherries
1 bunch of pink summer wildflowers
1 bunch of blue or purple wildflowers
2 stems pink hydrangea

Deep in the American heartland, where a patchwork of wildflower prairies and meadowlands form the iconic Great Plains, native prairie plants such as wild plums, chokeberries and wild grapes have always been prized for their inherent beauty as well as unique culinary potential. Discovered long ago by the Plains Indians, these wild plants and trees make distinctive jams, jellies, and wine – as well as beautiful decorations – a variety of simple gifts from the land. Inspired by the abundance of summer, this wreath of wild cherries, plums and wildflowers pays homage to the traditions and landscape of the American Midwest.

WILDFLOWER PLUM

HOW-TO *instructions*

1 Wrap the bark wire around the wreath to create a loop for hanging.
2 Create a base layer of ribbon using the ruched ribbon technique.
3 Using the straight wire, pierce the plums near the center, stringing 4 together.
4 Place the plum garland across the wreath, spacing the plums to cover the top and sides.
5 Wrap the ends of the wire around the wreath, securing them tightly in back. Cut the excess wire.
6 Working in horizontal rows, continue adding plum garlands in this manner until the entire wreath is covered.
7 Using the straight wire, string 6 – 7 grape tomatoes together and wrap the garlands across the plums, twisting the ends of the wire in back.
8 Continue adding grape tomato garlands until the entire wreath is covered.
9 Wire 3 black cherries to the wood pick, using the wire to pierce each cherry near the middle, wrapping the end to the wood pick.
10 Insert the cherry clusters in and around the wreath, including the inside and outside borders.
11 Add the wildflowers by inserting small bunches (e.g., 3 – 4 stems together) in the water picks and placing them evenly throughout the wreath.

DESIGN *note*

Substitute another kind of flower
– e.g. pink and purple statice –
if wildflowers are not available
or are not in season.

Across the gentle rolling fields and wildflower meadows in the shadow of Mt. Rainier, the charming daisy carpets the foothills in summertime with infinite swaths of bright and cheery blooms. While sometimes maligned for its humble nature and profusion of delicate (yet prolific) white flowers, the daisy always inspires and delights us with an incomparable sweetness and charm. This simple wreath of daisies and wildflower grasses celebrates the cheerful disposition and enduring appeal of the daisy – a lovely symbol of summer and modest beauty.

MEADOW DAISIES

WHAT *you'll need*

HOW-TO *instructions*

TOOLS: Bark wire
Clippers
Wire cutters
Scissors

MATERIALS:
1 21-inch floral foam wreath
10 bunches of daisies
1 bunch variegated pittosporum
2 bunches of field grass

DESIGN *note*

As an alternative technique for making the daisy wreath, wire a floral foam garland to a grapevine form, continuing with steps 3 – 8.

1 Wrap the bark wire around the wreath to create a loop for hanging.
2 Soak the floral foam wreath in water until it is completely saturated.
3 Cut small pieces of the pittosporum and insert them throughout the wreath to create a light base layer.
4 Cut the daisy stems into single pieces about 4 – 6-inches in length.
5 Working side to side across the wreath, insert daisies to cover the sides and top of the wreath, tucking the shorter ends near the sides.
6 Continue adding daisies, working in rows, creating a dense, rounded form, covering the entire wreath.
7 Insert the field grass into the form, focusing on the interior and outside edges.
8 Hang the wreath and insert additional daisies, as needed, to complete the design.

I n the picturesque Italian hill-side village of Montalcino, famous for its medieval castle, quaint architecture, and Brunello wine, our friends' farm overlooks rolling hills and countryside, including colorful fields of sunflowers and lavender. From an idyllic vantage point on an ancient stone terrace, situated under a pergola of grape vines and lemon topiaries, it's possible to catch the gentle breeze that blows through the olive groves and makes the sunflowers dance. This wreath is inspired by splendid summers in Montalcino, the incredible landscape of Tuscany and languid days sitting on the terrace, sipping a Negroni with dear friends.

WHAT *you'll need*

TOOLS: Bark wire
Straight wire (thinner gauge)
Clippers
Wire cutters
Scissors
6-inch wired wood picks
4-inch water picks

SUNFLOWERS UNDER THE TUSCAN SUN

MATERIALS:

1 21-inch floral foam wreath form
1 bunch variegated pittosporum
1 bunch olive branches
6 bunches mini sunflowers
8 bunches mini sunflower poms
1 pound purple grapes
30 lemons
10 stems of wild honeysuckle
(or similar vines)
10 yellow begonia blossoms
1 bunch green trailing ivy

DESIGN *note*

Create movement and depth by inserting a few longer stems of sunflower poms so that they float above the design.

HOW-TO *instructions*   2 Medium   3-5 D

1 Wrap the bark around the wreath to create a loop for hanging.
2 Soak the floral foam wreath until it is completely saturated.
3 Cut the olive branches into 6-inch lengths and insert a few pieces in the form, focusing on the inside and outside edges, reserving at least ½ bunch for later.
4 Cut the mini-sunflowers into 4 – 6-inch lengths and insert the stems evenly throughout the wreath so that they float a few inches above the form.
5 Clip the sunflower poms into individual pieces and place them in and around the wreath to cover the entire surface.
6 Wire small clusters of purple grapes to the wood picks and insert them evenly.
7 Using the straight wire, pierce the lemons, stringing two together, wrapping the ends of the wire together in back to secure the garland. Cut the excess wire.
8 Working in rows, continue adding strings of lemon in this manner until the entire wreath is covered, nestling them in and around the sunflowers.
9 Add the honeysuckle vine, weaving the vine in and around the sunflowers.
10 Insert small clusters of begonia blossoms into the water tubes.
11 As a finishing touch, tuck in the remaining pieces of olive branch foliage and add the greening trailing ivy to define the inner and outer borders.

WHAT *you'll need*

TOOLS: Bark wire
Boullion wire
Straight wire (thinner gauge)
Clippers
Wire cutters
Scissors
6-inch wired wood picks
4-inch water tubes

MATERIALS:
1 16-inch square grapevine wreath
1 ½ yards of fuchsia/red organza
4 pints of strawberries
5 pounds of red/purple grapes
(fresh or faux)
1 pints of red cherry tomatoes
1 small bunch of cherry blossom branches
1 bunch of green ivy

In Old Town Alexandria, Virginia near Washington, D.C. where I now live, spring is always an inspiration. Although it sometimes seems slow to arrive, peeking out in fits and starts while winter retains a lingering grasp, one day it gains momentum and becomes unstoppable, bursting forth in exuberant, spectacular fashion. The most obvious sign of spring in Washington, D.C. is the beloved cherry blossoms that ring the Tidal Basin in a profusion of pink petal clouds. So delicate and ephemeral, they symbolize the fleeting beauty of life and the promise of hope and renewal of spring. During cherry blossom season, I try to conjure up spring by planting the large urns flanking my front door with a mix of colorful blooms as soon as the weather permits. I like to add little strawberry plants to the mix, tucking these creeping, low-growing plants under the showier blossoms and foliage. The dainty flowers and long shoots spill over the edge, creating flowing vines and ruby red fruit. An iconic symbol in art through the ages, the strawberry represents perfection, purity and innocence. So when they are used together, the symbolic strawberry and iconic cherry blossoms create a lovely statement of spring, inspiring this design--the "strawberry blossom wreath" of fruit and flowers in the spring spirit.

| STRAWBERRY BLOSSOM

HOW-TO *instructions*   3 Expert   3-5 D

1   To create the base layer, cut the organza into a continuous 12-inch length and wrap it around the grapevine frame.

2   Wrap the bark wire around the wreath form to create a loop for hanging.

3   Add bunches of fresh (or faux) grapes by positioning across the sides and top of the wreath, binding them with the paddle wire.

4   Continue adding grapes until the entire wreath is covered.

5   Using the straight wire, create small, individual garlands of strawberries by stringing 3 together.

6   Working in rows, place the strawberry garlands across the top of the wreath, leaving space between each strawberry.
Wrap the wire ends to the back and tie securely.

7   Continue adding strawberries until the entire wreath is covered.

8   Create similar strings of cherry tomato garlands by stringing 5 together on the straight wire.

9   Position the tomato garlands evenly around the wreath, tying the ends securely in back.

10 Cut the cherry blossom branches into small 2 – 3-inch pieces and insert in water-filled picks.

11 Add the blossoms in and around the wreath.

12 As a finishing touch, wire small pieces of ivy to the wood picks, placing them primarily on the outside and inside edges.

On an early morning swing through the Old Town Farmers' Market this spring, as I gathered my usual produce and flowers for the week, I noticed that my salad ingredients (lettuce, French beans, grapes and basil) matched up nicely with my floral selections (hellebores, succulents and green ivy). The textures and colors blended well together and evoked the mood of early spring. So I made a quick decision to ditch plans for a salad that evening and turned the combination into this wreath – a spring green salad mix of seasonal produce and blooms.

SPRING GREEN SALAD

WHAT *you'll need*

TOOLS: Bark wire
Bind wire
Paddle wire
Clippers
Wire cutters
6-inch wired wood picks
4-inch water picks

MATERIALS:
1 18-inch grapevine wreath
2 pounds of fresh (or faux) grapes
5 heads of butter lettuce,
9 small succulents
1 bunch green hellebores
1 pound of French green beans
Green trailing ivy

HOW-TO *instructions*

1 Wrap the wreath form with bark wire to create a loop for hanging.
2 Using the wired wood picks, insert sprigs of ivy into the wreath form to create a light base layer.
3 Position the lettuce evenly around the wreath, securing the heads with the wood picks and inserting them into the grapevine frame.
4 Add succulents in the same manner, inserting them in and around the lettuce to cover the wreath.
5 Using the wood picks, wire bundles of grapes and insert them throughout the wreath to create a balanced and natural effect.
6 Cut small pieces of hellebores and insert them in water picks, placing the flowers so that they float above the lettuce and succulents.
7 Create several small garlands of bundled green beans with the bind wire, leaving about 5-inches of space between each bundle.
8 Weave the bundles in and around the wreath, focusing on the inside and outside edges.
9 Insert a few additional sprigs of ivy as a finishing touch.

DESIGN *note*

Mist the wreath with water and keep in a cool place to increase the longevity of the design.

For this iteration of the spring green salad wreath, I used fresh lettuce and ferns accented with hosta and ivy leaves from the garden. The fresh green palette and mix of textures displayed on a rustic cottage gate creates the feeling of "apres la pluie" – after the rain – when the garden glistens with morning dew.

HOW-TO *instructions*

1. Wrap the frame with bark wire to create a loop for hanging.
2. Using the wood picks, wire small pieces of ivy and insert in and around the wreath to create a light base layer.
3. Using the straight wire, pierce the head of lettuce near the root and lay across the wreath.
4. Wrap the wire ends to the back, twisting tightly to secure. Cut the excess wire. Continue adding lettuce in this manner until the entire wreath is covered.
5. Working left to right in rows around the wreath, add ferns, hosta and ivy, wiring the foliage to wood picks, interspersing the greenery throughout the wreath.

| LETTUCE & FERNS

WHAT *you'll need*

TOOLS: Bark wire
Straight wire (thinner gauge)
6-inch wired wood picks

MATERIALS:
1 18-inch grapevine wreath
8 heads of lettuce
Woodland ferns
Hosta leaves
Ivy

DESIGN *note*

Mist the finished wreath with water to extend its longevity and spray with "leaf shine" to add a luminous sheen.

WHAT *you'll need*

TOOLS: Bark wire
Bullion wire
Paddle wire
Straight wire (thinner gauge)
Clippers
Wire cutters
Scissors
Wired wood picks

MATERIALS:
1 18-inch straw wreath
1 pounds of mixed jalapeno peppers
  (red and green)
5 bunches of faux red berries
1 bag of fresh cranberries
1 pound of crabapples
1 bunch of green holly

This festive wreath of unusual textures and materials is inspired by traditional holiday colors and seasonal peppers, berries, crab apples and greens – with a Texan twist. During the holidays, my Lone Star state friends serve a potent drink made of jalapenos and cranberries, a perky cocktail with a rough and tumble cowboy kick. The flavors of peppers and cranberries blend well in the drink – and work surprisingly well as decorative elements, too. Here is a recipe for a Texas pepper wreath, inspired by Texas heat and hospitality and my friends in the Dallas, Ft. Worth, Houston and San Antonio garden clubs.

WINTER PEPPERS & BERRIES

HOW-TO *instructions*

1 Wrap the bark wire around the wreath to create a loop for hanging.
2 Cut the berries into 4-inch pieces and bundle 3 pieces together with the bullion wire, creating small "bouquets" of berries.
3 Working left to right, lay individual bundles of berries across the wreath in rows, wrapping the paddle wire around the base 2-3 times to secure them.
4 Continue adding berry bundles in this manner, working in rows across the wreath, covering the entire front and sides of the wreath in berries.
5 Using the straight wire, pierce the hot peppers, stringing 4 – 5 together to create garlands.
6 Wrap the hot pepper garland loosely over the berries, creating dimension, tying the wire together in the back to secure the garland.
7 Continue adding the hot pepper garlands, spacing them a few inches apart, until the entire wreath is covered.
8 Create similar garlands of cranberries by stringing 5 together and wrapping them around the berries to create an additional layer of texture.
9 Add the crabapples by inserting one end of the wired wood pick into the fruit and the other into the straw frame.
10 As a finishing touch, wire clippings of holly into the wreath using the wired picks in a random, yet balanced pattern.

With a vivid green color in every shade of lime and emerald hue, green peppers are an ideal choice for a variety of seasonal wreath designs. Long-lasting, with interesting spiky forms, they work well together alone or with other fruits, flowers and vegetables. Here, I've used a grapevine diamond form to create a version of a lime green wreath featuring mixed green peppers from the market. The base is a layer of ruched moss green ribbon with layers of wired peppers, finished with lime green alstromeria blossoms.

WHAT *you'll need*

TOOLS: Bark wire
Straight wire (thinner gauge)
Bullion wire
Clippers
Wire cutters
Scissors
6-inch wired wood picks
4-inch water picks

GREEN PEPPER DIAMOND

MATERIALS:

1 18-inch diamond wreath frame
(wire or grape vine)
1 roll of 1 ½ inch moss green ribbon
30 emerald green chile peppers
30 lime green banana peppers
1 pound of goat peppers (thin green pepper)
1 bunch lime green alstromeria

HOW-TO *instructions*

1 Wrap the bark wire around the wreath to create a loop for hanging.
2 Create a ribbon base layer using the ruched ribbon technique.
3 Pierce the emerald green peppers with the straight wire, stringing 2 together.
4 Lay the pepper garland across the wreath, wrap the ends around and twist together in back. Cut the excess wire.
5 Continue adding pepper garlands in this manner, spacing them evenly.
6 Using the straight wire, create banana pepper garlands, stringing 2 together.
7 Lay the banana pepper garlands across the wreath, wrap around and twist.
8 Continue adding banana pepper garlands until the entire wreath is covered.
9 Using the bullion wire, create garlands of goat peppers, stringing 3 together.
10 Wrap the goat pepper garland around the wreath form, weaving these peppers and around the other materials.
11 Continue adding goat pepper garlands until the entire wreath is covered.
12 As a finishing touch, cut small pieces of green alstromeria and place in water picks, inserting them around the wreath.

The sweet Virginia bluebell, an ephemeral flower with bell-shaped sky blue flowers is a [su]re sign that spring has sprung in the Old Domi[ni]on. In my garden, this hardy perennial plant first [ap]pears in March with small pink buds before the [bl]ue blossoms emerge April. For this variation of [th]e green pepper wreath, I've added apples and [bl]ue bells to make a garden-style wreath in the [bl]ue and green palette of early spring.

HOW-TO *instructions*

3 Expert   5-7 D

1 Wrap the bark wire around the wreath, double it, to create a loop for hanging.
2 Create a ribbon base layer using the ruched ribbon technique.
3 Pierce the green apple with the straight wire, stringing 2 together.
4 Lay the apple garland across the wreath, wrap the ends around and twist together in back. Cut the excess wire.
5 Continue adding apple garlands in this manner, spacing them evenly.
6 Using the straight wire, create banana pepper garlands, stringing 2 together, piercing them in the middle.
7 Wire the banana pepper garlands to the form, placing them around the apples, covering the entire wreath.
8 Working in rows, continue adding the okra and green chili peppers in this manner, building up texture around the wreath.
9 Cut the blue bells and insert them in water picks.
10 Place the blue bells in and around the wreath so that the flowers float above the apples and peppers.
11 As a finishing touch, tuck in sprigs of ivy, focusing on the interior and outside edges.

GREEN PEPPERS & BLUE BELLS

WHAT *you'll need*

TOOLS: Bark wire
Bullion wire
Straight wire (thinner gauge)
Clippers
Wire cutters
Scissors
4-inch water picks

MATERIALS:
1 18-inch grapevine wreath
1 roll of 1 ½-inch green ribbon
30 green apples
2 pounds of banana peppers
3 pounds of okra
2 pounds of green chili peppers
Virginia blue bells
Green trailing ivy

Akey component of French floral design is the use of folded and manipulated leaves, including techniques that resemble ribbons and pleated fabric. Inspired by haute couture and enhanced by the rich French floral art tradition, these techniques are perfect for creating innovative bouquet and wreath designs. Here, I've used the long-lasting aspidistra leaf – called the "iron leaf" in Victorian times for its durability and longevity – to create an elegant seasonal display. The shiny green wreath makes a striking statement on a coordinating or contrasting door.

WHAT *you'll need*

TOOLS: Bark wire
Bullion wire
Paddle wire
Wire cutters
Scissors
6-inch wired wood picks (optional)

MATERIALS:
1 18-inch grapevine (or straw) wreath
10 bunches of green aspidistra

DESIGN *note 1*

Spray the finished wreath with "leaf shine" to give the leaves a glossy finish.

DESIGN *note 2*

Other long-lasting leaves and grasses, including flax, magnolia and lemon leaf salal can be used to create similar patterns and variations of this wreath design.

RIBBON LEAF

HOW-TO *instructions*

1 Wrap the wreath with the bark wire to create a loop for hanging.
2 Prepare the leaves by cutting them into a continuous spiral.
3 Fold the center piece of the leaf down to create a loop.
4 Holding the end of the cut leaf, wrap it in and around the loop to create a ribbon-like effect, tying it with bullion wire and securing it to the stem.
5 Continue creating ribbon leaves in this manner.
6 Working in rows from side to side across the wreath, insert the stems into the form.
7 Continue adding rows of folded leaves in this manner until the entire wreath is covered.
8 Using the paddle wire, wrap the base of each row to secure the leaves tightly to the frame, continuing around the wreath.
9 Secure the paddle wire to the bark wire.

WHAT *you'll need*

TOOLS: Bark wire
Stapler
Floral u-pins
Paddle wire
Leaf shine spray

MATERIALS:

1 24-inch straw wreath
30 bunches of green
   aspidistra leaves

For this variation of the ribbon leaf wreath, inspired by Parisian haute couture and the designs of iconic Japanese fashion designer Issey Miyake, I created a pleated green leaf wreath of aspidistra leaves that are pinned in rows around a straw wreath form. The effect is simple, yet refined and can be used for a variety of occasions throughout the year.

PLEATED GREEN LEAF

HOW-TO *instructions*   2 Medium   2 W +

1 Wrap the bark wire around the wreath to create a loop for hanging.
2 Fold the aspidistra leaf in half, stapling the point and base of the leaf together.
3 Continue folding and stapling all of the leaves.
4 Trim the stems to 2-inch lengths.
5 Working left to right in rows across the wreath, pin the base of the leaf to the straw form.
6 After each row is complete, wrap the paddle wire around the stems to secure.
7 Continue adding rows of leaves until the entire wreath is covered, taking care to pin them close to the base of the preceding row.
8 Spray the finished wreath with leaf shine for a polished look.

TIP

Cut the ends of the aspidistra stems
 on the diagonal to form a point.
 If the stems are too short,
wire the leaves to wood picks.

WHAT *you'll need*

TOOLS: Barked wire
Bullion wire
Paddle wire
Straight wire (thinner gauge)
Wire cutters
Clippers
Scissors
6-inch wired wood picks
4-inch water picks

MATERIALS:
1 18-inch grapevine wreath
1 roll of 1 ½-inch purple ribbon
100 mini red/purple potatoes = 8 – 12 bags
15 stems of pink wild sweet pea vine (substitute dendrobium orchids or jasmine vine)
12 stems fuchsia wild roses (or spray roses)
1 pint black cherries

There are many places of beauty throughout the world, but the dawning of spring in the Pacific Northwest surely must rank among the top for its distinctive, breathtaking splendor of flowering branches, daffodils, tulips, azaleas and giant rhododendrons that emerge from the gray fog and mist. In early May, one of my favorite sights is the carpet of violas that blanket the aptly named Violet Prairie near my family home in Southwest Washington State. By the height of summer, the landscape is covered with a riotous tangle of wild sweet pea and blackberry vines, characterized by bright pink flowers, ripe fruit and sage green vines. This "primrose potato" wreath is inspired by the beauty and bounty of a Seattle spring with purple potatoes from the market and sweet peas, blackberry vines and roses from the garden.

PRIMROSE POTATO & SWEET PEAS

HOW-TO *instructions* (2 Medium) [5-7 D]

1. Wrap bark wire around the wreath to create a loop for hanging.
2. Create a ribbon base layer using the ruched ribbon technique.
3. Attach the ribbon garland to the front of the grape vine form, tying it to the edges with the paddle wire.
4. Using the straight wire, pierce the potatoes, stringing 3 together.
5. Wrap the string of wired potatoes across the front of the wreath form, twisting and securing the wire tightly in back. Cut the excess wire.
6. Add the potato strings in rows, working around the frame until the entire wreath form is covered.
7. Using the bullion wire and wired wood picks, wire 2 – 3 cherries together by piercing the center and/or tying the stems together, creating small bundles.
8. Attach the cherry bundles to the frame in a natural pattern, inserting the wood picks both inside and outside across the wreath.
9. Cut the wild sweet pea vines into 10 – 12-inch lengths, inserting them in the water picks.
10. As a finishing touch, add the sweet pea vines, inserting the water picks into the frame, weaving them around the wreath.

WHAT *you'll need*

TOOLS: Bullion wire
Bark wire
Straight wire (thinner gauge)
Clippers
Wire cutters
Scissors
6-inch wired wood picks
4-inch water picks

MATERIALS:
1 18-inch grapevine wreath
1 roll of 1 ½ yellow satin ribbon
7 yellow bell peppers
35 apricots
25 lemons
2 pints yellow cherries
1 bunch yellow spray garden roses
1 bunch euonymus
1 bunch "love in a puff" vine

For those of us who are Seattle natives, the Pike Place Market has always been a special place full of quintessential Northwest flavor and fun. Long before it became a movie backdrop and tourist destination, the market has held special allure: from the flying fish and colorful seasonal produce and flowers to inspiring local cuisine – not to mention the most amazing views across Puget Sound – the market is truly an enjoyable, special experience. This wreath features Pike Place Market bounty from amazing farmers' gardens with a golden summer theme.

| YELLOW PEPPERS & APRICOTS

HOW-TO *instructions*   3-5 D

1   Wrap the bark wire around the wreath to create a loop for hanging.
2   Create the yellow ribbon base layer using the ruched ribbon technique.
3   Using the straight wire, pierce the yellow peppers and position them evenly on the wreath. Wrap the ends of the wires around the back, tying them securely.
4   Add the apricots by stringing 2 together on the straight wire. Wrap the wire ends around the wreath, securing them in the back.
5   Working in rows, continue adding strings of apricots until the wreath is evenly covered.
6   Add the lemons in the same manner – stringing them individually with the straight wire, placing them to fill in gaps.
7   Cut the garden roses into 4-inch pieces, insert in the water picks and place evenly around the wreath.
8   Wire small pieces of variegated euonymus to the wood picks and insert them in and around the wreath, including the inside and outside edges.
9   Cut the "love in a puff" vine into 10 – 12-inch pieces and insert in water picks.
10 As a finishing touch, insert the vine into the wreath, wrapping it across the surface to float above the other elements.

The color purple has long been associated with royalty, nobility, luxury, power and ambition. It also represents creativity, wisdom, grandeur, mystery, independence and magic. Purple was my Louisiana great-grandmother's favorite color: she loved purple pansies, sweet violets and irises and collected lavender glassware and several sets of china with a purple and violet theme – many pretty things that I am now lucky to own. So it's no wonder that I also love purple in its full range of hues and view the purple orchid as one of my favorite flowers. When mixed with purple vegetables, including cabbages and turnips, the purple orchid takes on a regal note and reminds me of sweet violets and vintage gardens with a Louisiana twist.

PURPLE CABBAGE & TURNIPS

WHAT *you'll need*

TOOLS:
Bark wire
Bullion wire
Straight wire (heavier gauge)
Straight wire (thinner gauge)
Clippers
Scissors
Wire cutters
6-inch wired wood picks
4-inch water picks

MATERIALS:
1 18-inch grape vine wreath
1 roll of purple 1 ½-inch ribbon
7 purple cabbages
25 purple turnips
5 stems purple dendrobium orchids
1 pint black cherries

HOW-TO *instructions*

2 Medium   3-5 D

1 Wrap the bark wire around the frame, doubling it, to create a loop for hanging.

2 Create a base layer of purple ribbon using the ruched ribbon technique.

3 Using the heavy straight wire, pierce the purple cabbages, positioning them evenly around the wreath, tying the wires securely together in back.

4 Next, string 2 turnips together using the heavy gauge straight wire and wrap them across the top of the frame, adjacent to the cabbages, securing the ends of the wires together in back. Cut the excess wire.

5 Continue adding turnips until the entire wreath is covered, creating a balanced presentation.

6 Add a layer of black cherries by stringing 5 together using the thinner straight wire, placing them over the top of the cabbages and turnips, wiring them together in back. Trim excess wires.

7 Cut the dendrobium orchids into small pieces, insert in water picks and then into the wreath form, covering the entire wreath with orchid blooms.

One of the most cherished traditions in Old Town Alexandria, Virginia is the annual Scottish Christmas Walk that celebrates Alexandria's Scottish heritage. The quaint parade that winds through the historic streets features old cars and local politicians, bagpipes and kilts, and plaid and heather-clad residents marching proudly behind their namesake clans. A highlight of the parade is always the dogs – Scotty terriers, bulldogs, Irish wolfhounds – a full panoply of beloved British Isle breeds. But perhaps my favorite part of the parade is when the burly guys dressed as Celtic warriors join in, wrapped in burlap togas and woolen blankets, waving ancient weapons and drinking from deer-hide flasks, dressed to conquer but full of whisky, their inebriated antics adding flavor and character to the day. This wreath of cabbage, heather and hellebores ushers in the holiday season in Old Town Alexandria with a nod to our Scottish heritage.

CABBAGES, HEATHER & CAMELLIA

WHAT *you'll need*

TOOLS: Bark wire
Straight wire (thinner gauge)
Straight wire (heavier gauge)
Clippers
Wire cutters
Scissors
6-inch wired wood picks
4-inch water picks

MATERIALS:
1 18-inch grapevine wreath
10 stems of purple kale cabbage
3 purple kohlrabi cabbage
10 sugar beets
1 bunch of grapes
2 bunches of heather
1 bunch of blooming camellia
Green trailing ivy

HOW-TO *instructions*

 2 Medium   5-7 D

1 Wrap the bark wire around the wreath to create a loop for hanging.
2 Wire short sprigs of ivy to the wood picks and insert into the wreath to create a light base layer of greenery.
3 Trim the kale cabbage stems to about 3-inches, insert the wired wood pick into the stem, and place the cabbages evenly around the wreath.
4 Next, position the kohlrabi on the wreath, using the heavy straight wire to pierce the cabbages, and then wrap and tie the wire ends in the back.
5 Using the straight wire (thinner gauge), pierce the sugar beets and attach them to the wreath in the same manner, spacing them evenly around the wreath.
6 Take small clusters of grapes and attach them to the wired wood picks, placing them in the wreath to create a balanced presentation.
7 Bundle 3 sprigs of heather together with the wired wood pick and insert them in and around the wreath, focusing on the inside and outside edges.
8 Insert the camellia blossoms and foliage in the water picks and place them throughout the wreath.
9 As a finishing touch, tuck in sprigs of ivy using the wired wood picks.

The key to a great apple pie, according to my husband Bob, is a hand-made Fannie Farmer crust, light and flaky with mix of apples and spices: sweet and tart, not too juicy but not dry either. My grandmother would say that a few pear slices tucked into the mix add a delightful sweetness to the dessert, a pie that is known to garner enthusiastic requests for a second slice. This wreath, a combination of autumn apples and pears with ivy is designed to be the wreath equivalent of the ultimate apple pie.

WHAT *you'll need*

TOOLS: Bark wire
　　　Straight wire (thinner gauge)
　　　6-inch wired wood picks
　　　Bullion wire
　　　Clippers
　　　Wire cutters
　　　Scissors

MATERIALS:
　　　1 roll of 1½-inch moss green ribbon
　　　1 18-inch grapevine wreath
　　　8 – 9 bags gala (or honey crisp) apples
　　　50 small pears (fresh or faux)
　　　1 bunch of green bush ivy

| PEARS & APPLES

HOW-TO *instructions*

1　Wrap the wreath frame with the bark wire to create a loop for hanging.
2　Create a green ribbon base layer using the ruched ribbon technique.
3　Using the straight wire, pierce the apples and string 4 together.
4　Place the apple garland across the top of the wreath, wrapping the wire ends around and securing tightly in the back.
5　Working in rows, continue adding apple garlands to the wreath until the entire wreath is covered, securing the wires in the back. Cut excess wire with the wire cutters.
6　Wire the small pears in the same manner, stringing 4 together.
7　Place the pear garlands evenly throughout the wreath, laying them across the top and tying the wire ends in the back, cutting the excess wire.
8　Create small bundles of ivy by binding 3 – 4 (3-inch pieces) together with the bullion wire.
9　As a finishing touch, wire the ivy bundles to the wood picks and insert them in and around the wreath.

DESIGN *note*

Spray the fruit with liquid floor wax to keep it fresh longer.

For a touch of spring, nothing compares to daffodils -- so breathtaking as a single flower or experienced en masse as large swaths of spring happiness fluttering and dancing in the breeze. Daffodils have always been one of my favorite flowers since they can be enjoyed in so many ways – in the garden, in mixed bouquets, in single bedside bud vases. Here, I've incorporated daffodils in a wreath of golden apples and fingerling potatoes – a composition designed to resemble spring bulbs and the bright golden colors and flowers of the season.

WHAT *you'll need*

TOOLS: Bark wire
Bullion wire
Straight wire (thinner gauge)
Clippers
Wire cutters
Scissors
6-inch wired wood picks
4-inch water picks

GOLDEN APPLES, POTATOES & DAFFODILS

MATERIALS:

1 18-inch diamond shape grapevine wreath
1 roll of 1 ½-inch yellow ribbon
50 golden apples
3 pounds of mini fingerling potatoes
2 bunches of white daffodil, yellow centers
1 bunch of yellow leucadendron
Green trailing ivy

HOW-TO *instructions*

1 Wrap the bark wire around the wreath, doubling it, to create a loop for hanging.
2 Create a ribbon garland base layer using the ruched ribbon technique.
3 Pierce a golden apple with the straight wire, stringing two together.
4 Lay the apple strings across the top of the wreath, wrap the wire end around and twist them together in the back.
5 Work in rows, adding apple strings until the entire wreath is covered.
6 Next, pierce the fingerling potatoes with the straight wire, stringing 4 together.
7 Place a potato string across the top of the apples, wrap the wire ends around and twist them together in the back.
8 Continue adding potato strings, placing them evenly around the wreath.
9 Wire sprigs of yellow leucadendron to the wood picks and insert them in and around the wreath.
10 Insert the daffodils in water picks and place them so that the flowers float above the wreath.
11 As a finishing touch, add sprigs of ivy using the wired wood picks, focusing on the inside and outside edges.

DESIGN *note*

Add an additional apple at each corner to define the diamond shape.

For this variation of the green apple wreath, I was inspired by the wild sweet pea vines that grow in abundance in Pacific Northwest gardens, along the trails and roadsides, and near the ocean in summer. The bright fuchsia bloom on a sage green vine is the perfect counterpoint to regimented rows of shiny lime green apples; they add a touch of wildness and whimsy to the classical form.

GREEN APPLES & WILD SWEET PEAS

WHAT *you'll need*

TOOLS: Bark wire
Straight wire (thinner gauge)
Bullion wire
Paddle wire
Clippers
Wire cutters
Scissors
4-inch water picks

MATERIALS:
1 18-inch grapevine wreath
2 bunches evergreen fir tips
90 granny smith apples
3 bunches of wild sweet pea vines

HOW-TO *instructions*

 2 Medium   3-5 D

1 Wrap the bark wire around the wreath, doubling it, to create a loop for hanging.

2 Cut the fir into small 4-inch pieces, bundling 3 together with the bullion wire at the base.

3 Lay the fir bundles across the wreath form in rows and wrap with paddle wire.

4 Holding the paddle wire, continue to add rows of fir bundles, wrapping at the base to secure, overlapping the rows to hide the wire, continuing until the entire form is covered.

5 Using the straight wire, pierce the apple, stringing 4 together.

6 Lay the apple garland across the wreath form, wrap the ends around, twisting together in the back to secure. Clip the excess wire.

7 Working in even rows around the wreath, continue adding apple garlands in this manner until the entire wreath is covered.

8 Insert lengths of sweet pea vines in the water picks and place in and around the wreath to create a balanced presentation.

According to ancient lore, the winter-blooming hellebore (also known as the Christmas rose) has magical properties – ostensibly providing protection to those around it, driving away an unpleasant atmosphere and replacing it with tranquility. Known for its delicate green and white (or purple) blooms, the hellebore always adds a touch of classic simplicity and fresh holiday cheer in the middle of winter. In this wreath, I've paired green hellebores with green apples for a fanciful, seasonal study in green.

GREEN APPLES & HELLEBORES

WHAT *you'll need*

TOOLS:
Bark wire
Straight wire (thinner gauge)
Clippers
Wire cutters
Scissors
6-inch wired wood picks
4-inch water picks

MATERIALS:
1 21-inch oval grapevine wreath
1 roll of 1 ½-inch emerald green ribbon
70 green Granny Smith apples
2 bunches of variegated israeli ruscus
1 bunch eucalyptus
2 bunches green hellebores

HOW-TO *instructions*

 2 Medium   5-7 D

1 Wrap the bark wire around the wreath, doubling it, to create a loop for hanging.
2 Create a base layer of emerald green ribbon using the ruched ribbon technique.
3 Using the straight wire, pierce the green apples, stringing 3 together.
4 Lay the apple garland across the top of the wreath, spacing the apples evenly.
5 Wrap the ends of the wire to the back of the wreath, tying them together to secure.
6 Working in rows around the wreath, add the apple garlands in this manner until the entire wreath is covered.
7 Wire sprigs of variegated israeli ruscus to the wood picks and insert them in and around the wreath.
8 Add sprigs of eucalyptus in the same manner to create additional texture.
9 Cut pieces of hellebore and insert them in the water picks.
10 Add the hellebore blossoms as a finishing touch, inserting them in the wreath to float above the apples and greenery.

WHAT *you'll need*

TOOLS: Bark wire
Boullion wire
Clippers
Wire cutters
scissors
6-inch wired wood picks

MATERIALS:
1 15-inch floral foam heart wreath
1 roll 1 ½-inch pink ribbon
1 small sheet of pink organza
1 bunch of variegated pittosporum
1 dozen pale pink roses
10 stems pink peonies
1 bunch pink alstromeria
1 bunch pink spray carnations
1 bunch antique pink spray carnations
2 bunches pink gerbera daisies
Green trailing ivy

In the supernatural Chinese play "The Peony Pavilion," written in 1598, a young woman falls asleep in in her family's garden and has vivid dreams of falling in love with a dashing young suitor. When she awakens, she pines away for her mythical dream lover until the day she dies. Then, miraculously, the suitor stops by the garden where the heroine is buried. He sees her portrait and falls deeply in love. She appears as a ghost and convinces him to disinter her so that she can come back to life and be re-united with her long lost love. This romantic love story that transcends time and reality takes place against the backdrop of a beautiful peony garden. Here, a pink heart wreath of pink spring flowers and majestic pink peonies sends a message of beauty and transcendent love.

| PINK ROSE & PEONY HEART

HOW-TO *instructions*   5-7 D

1. Wrap the bark wire around the wreath to create a loop for hanging.
2. Soak the floral foam wreath in water until it is completely saturated.
3. Insert sprigs of variegated pittosporum in the wreath, covering the form in a light layer.
4. Cut the roses to 4 – 5-inch lengths and place them evenly around the wreath.
5. Add the peonies and gerbera daisies in the same manner, inserting them in and around the wreath.
6. Next, insert the alstromeria, filling in the spaces around the peonies, daisies and roses.
7. Continue filling in the wreath with sprigs of carnations so that the entire wreath is covered in flowers.
8. Create 8 – 10 pieces of ruched ribbon (4 – 5-inches in length) using the technique, tucking them in among the flowers.
9. As a finishing touch, cut the organza into 4-inch squares, wire the middle to the wood picks and intersperse these organza "florets" throughout the wreath.

DESIGN *note*

Add a border of green ivy
as an optional touch.

The bluebird is a harbinger of happiness and a symbol of good luck in many cultures while butterflies are prized for their elegant, ephemeral beauty. Together, bluebirds and butterflies create a transformational message of optimism and lightness, exemplifying the garden in spring. In this wreath, vivid iris bluebirds, combined with orchid and clematis butterflies, mingle together on clouds of white hydrangea to make an inspirational seasonal display.

BLUEBIRDS & BUTTERFLIES

WHAT *you'll need*

TOOLS: Bark wire
Clippers
Wire cutters
Scissors
6-inch wired wood picks

MATERIALS:
1 21-inch floral foam wreath
1 bunch variegated pittosporum
10 stems white hydrangea
1 bunch viburnum
50 stems of cream roses
1 bunche purple iris
2 bunches tulips
1 bunch purple mokara orchids
1 bunch purple clematis
Purple lantana

HOW-TO *instructions*

1 Wrap the bark wire around the wreath to create a loop for hanging.
2 Soak the wreath form in water so that it is completely saturated.
3 Cut the pittosporum into small pieces and insert the stems in the wreath, creating a light base layer.
4 Working in drifts around the wreath, add the hydrangea, positioning them evenly, covering the entire wreath.
5 Add the roses, clustering 2 together, working from left to right in rows around the wreath.
6 Next, add sprigs of viburnum, blending them in throughout the wreath.
7 Cut the iris to 4 – 5-inch lengths and insert in the wreath, creating a "ribbon" effect with the placement of the flowers.
8 Add the tulips in the same manner, placing them throughout the wreath.
9 Place orchid sprigs so that they float above the wreath, focusing on the interior and outside edges.
10 As a finishing touch, insert sprigs of lantana to create additional texture and depth.

For this lavender and cream design, I took inspiration from the rhododendrons and lilac bushes that grew outside my childhood bedroom in Chehalis, Washington. These sweet flowers of the northwest spring – scented lilac, azaleas and rhododendron – are lovely together, evoking lavender and lace as well as a sense of nostalgic charm and simple elegance. Although this wreath works well as a festive greeting on a door or garden gate, perhaps it's best used as an indoor wreath, where its fleeting beauty and intoxicating scent can be most appreciated.

HOW-TO *instructions*

2
Medium

3 D

1 Wrap the bark wire around the wreath to create a loop for hanging.
2 Soak the wreath form in water so that it is completely saturated.
3 Cut sprigs of pittosporum and insert in the wreath to create a light base layer.
4 Add pieces of lilac, inserting them from side to side across the wreath, covering the sides and top.
5 Working in rows, continue adding the lilac until the entire wreath is covered.
6 Next, add the lavender rhododendron, spacing the flowers evenly among the lilac.
7 As a finishing touch, cut pieces of ivory rhododendron blooms and insert them into the form so that the flowers float in and around the lilac.

| LILAC RHODODENDRON

WHAT *you'll need*

TOOLS: Bark wire
Clippers
4-inch water picks

MATERIALS:
1 18-inch floral foam wreath
1 bunch of variegated pittosporum
3 bunches of lilac
1 bunch lavender rhododendron
1 bunch ivory rhododendron

Every year on the first Saturday in May, the melodious tones of "My Old Kentucky Home" waft across the lawns of Churchill Downs as thousands of people sing in unison, signaling the start of the Kentucky Derby, a beloved American tradition. As the trumpeter's call to post, summoning the horses to enter the starting gate, the festive hat-bedecked crowd turns briefly from their mint juleps to focus on the race and the quest for the coveted trophy and blanket of velvety roses that will adorn the winner. In 2018, the beautiful chestnut colt with the white blaze ("Justify") won the Kentucky Derby, the Preakness and the Belmont Stakes to become only the 13th horse in history to win the Triple Crown. This red rose wreath is inspired by the "run for the roses," iconic traditions and the quest for excellence.

WHAT *you'll need*

TOOLS: Bark wire
Paddle wire
Clippers
Wire cutters
Scissors
Boullion wire
6-inch wired wood picks

MATERIALS:
1 21-inch floral foam wreath
2 rolls of 2 ½-inch red velvet ribbon
1 roll of 1 ½-inch fuchsia ribbon
2 bunches (50 stems) of red roses
1 bunch (10 stems) fuchsia peonies
1 bunch fuchsia alstromeria
2 pints grape cherry tomatoes
1 large bunch of green ivy

| RUN FOR THE ROSES

HOW-TO *instructions*

1 Wrap the bark wire around the wreath to create a loop for hanging.
2 Soak the form in water until it is completely saturated.
3 Prepare the base layer by inserting small pieces of ivy to cover the entire surface of the wreath with a light layer of the greenery.
4 Use the paddle wire to create 15 velvet bows, 6-inches long, attach to the wood picks.
5 Insert the bows into the wreath, focusing on the inside and outside edges.
6 Cut the red roses into 4 – 5-inch pieces and place them evenly in and around the wreath, working from side to side to create "ribbons" of roses.
7 Insert the peonies in the wreath, spacing them evenly, focusing on a balanced presentation.
8 Cut the alstromeria into individual pieces and insert the florets to fill in spaces between the roses and peonies.
9 Using the wired wood picks, pierce 3 tomatoes together, wrapping the wire securely to the base.
10 Insert the picked tomatoes into the wreath so that they float slightly above the flowers, spreading them throughout the wreath.
11 For extra color and texture, insert the ruched ribbon using the wood picks.
12 As a finishing touch, add extra ivy, focusing on the inside and outside edges.

In southern style Virginia gardens, the "coral charm" peony and salmon pink azalea make charming companions, dazzling us with brilliant displays of color and ruffled petals that take center stage in May. When planted together, they are especially striking – a profusion of pink and coral petal perfection. In this garden remix wreath, I've added mini petunias and spray roses to create an intense, concentrated version of a Virginia garden in May.

WHAT *you'll need*

TOOLS: Bark wire
1 roll 1 ½-inch fuchsia ribbon
Bullion wire
6-inch wired picks
Clippers
Wire cutters

MATERIALS:
1 18-inch floral foam wreath
1 bunch variegated pittosporum
5 stems coral charm peony
1 bunche fuchsia azalea
1 bunch coral spray roses
10 – 12 mini petunia blossom

TIP

By inserting the roses at various angles in the wreath, it's possible to create a sense of energy and movement.

CORAL CHARM

HOW-TO *instructions*   3-5 D

1 Wrap the wreath form with the bark wire to create a loop for hanging.
2 Soak the wreath form in water until it is completely saturated.
3 Cut small pieces of pittosporum and insert them in the form, covering the sides and top of the wreath. Leave a couple of-inches between the foliage and the wreath base.
4 Cut the azalea branches into small pieces and insert them evenly around the wreath, leaving about 3 – 4-inches of space between the blossoms and the wreath.
5 Place the peonies around the wreath to create a balanced presentation.
6 Add the spray roses, cutting individual blossoms and inserting them in and around the wreath, covering the entire surface.
7 Insert clippings of coral and fuchsia petunias into the wreath so that they float above the other flowers.
8 For additional color and texture, add touches of ribbon using the ruched ribbon technique, tucking 4-inch pieces in the form with wired wood picks.

WHAT *you'll need*

TOOLS: Bark wire
Straight wire – thinner gauge
Bullion wire
Paddle wire
4-inch water picks
6-inch wired wood picks
Clippers
Wire cutters
Scissors

MATERIALS:
1 18-inch oval grapevine wreath
1 roll of 1 ½-inch fuchsia ribbon
8 bunches real (or faux) red grapes
15 red apples
15 purple plums
2 pints red cherries
2 stems purple vanda orchid
1 bunch fuchsia mokara orchid
2 bags purple pearl onions
1 bunch of holly
1 box of small fuchsia ornaments (optional)

This wreath of ruby fruit in a regal palette of violet, plum and purple tones is inspired by the jewels and gemstones – garnets, rubies and amethysts – most prized for their rare beauty and luminous color. Evocative of royalty, rich fabrics such as velvet and brocade and the color of Bordeaux wine, this wreath of fruit and flowers, accented with a few holiday baubles, evokes an opulent jewel and gemstone theme.

RUBY FRUIT
WINTER PLUMS, GRAPES & ORCHIDS

HOW-TO *instructions*

1   Wrap the bark wire around the wreath form to create a loop for hanging.
2   Create a base layer of fuchsia ribbon using the ruched ribbon technique.
3   Pierce the red apples with the straight wire, positioning them evenly around the wreath frame. Tie the wires by twisting them tightly in the back.
4   Add the purple plums in the same manner: placing the wired plums in and around the apples, securing the wire in the back.
5   Using the straight wire, string the cherries together, 5 in a row.
Wrap the cherry garland across the wreath, tying the wires in the back.
6   Add an accent layer of purple pearl onions by piercing 3 onions with the straight wire, placing the garland across the wreath, and tying the wires together in the back.
7   Cut individual blossoms of vanda orchids and insert them in the water picks. Add the orchid blooms around the wreath, placing them both near the inside and outside edges.
8   Cut small pieces of mokara orchids in the same manner, adding the water picks throughout the wreath.
9   Wrap small pieces of holly with the wired wood picks and insert them into the wreath as a finishing touch.
10   For a holiday look, add small fuchsia ornaments with the wired wood picks as a festive touch.

Sugarplums are a recurring theme during the holiday season where they have a prominent place in the classic Christmas tale "Twas the Night Before Christmas" and in the iconic "Dance of the Sugar Plum Fairy" from the Nutcracker Ballet. You might be surprised to learn that sugar plums are actually lowly prunes, albeit embellished with alcohol, almond paste and sugar to make them more palatable and less medicinal. Soaked overnight in port wine, stuffed with blanched almonds and rolled in sugar, this quaint British Christmas culinary tradition elevates the prune from humble status to a delectable and coveted sweet holiday treat. A wreath of aubergine plums and wine-colored hellebores conjures the magic and flavor of these classic sugarplums in the holiday tradition.

SUGARPLUMS & HELLEBORES

WHAT *you'll need*

TOOLS: Bark wire
Straight wire (thinner gauge)
1 roll of 1 ½-inch aubergine ribbon
Bullion wire
Clippers
Wire cutters
6-inch wired wood picks
4-inch water picks

MATERIALS:
1 21-inch oval grapevine wreath
100 red plums
2 bunches of purple hellebores
1 bunch red berries (e.g., ilex or hypericum berries)
1 bunch lemon leaf (salal) tips

HOW-TO *instructions*

1 Wrap the wreath form with the bark wire to create a loop for hanging.
2 Create a base layer of aubergine ribbon using the ruched ribbon technique.
3 Using the straight wire, pierce the plums, stringing 4 together.
4 Lay the plum garland across the wreath, wrap the wire ends around and secure tightly in back. Clip the excess wire.
5 Working in even rows around the wreath, add additional plum garlands in this manner until the entire form is covered.
6 Cut small pieces of hellebores, insert them in water picks and place the blooms evenly in and around the wreath.
7 Wire small pieces of red berries to the wood picks and insert them into the form so that they float above the plums and hellebores.
8 As a finishing touch, wire small pieces of lemon leaf to the wood picks and insert them in the wreath, focusing on the exterior and interior edges.

Cherry blossom season is the most beautiful time in Washington, D.C. when the entire city seems to be awash in a sea of delicate purple and pink petals. Like an Impressionist's paintbrush alighting on canvas, the cherry blossoms ring the Tidal Basin in clouds of cotton candy pink splendor. This wreath of potatoes and cherry blossoms (spuds and buds) is inspired by the colors and textures of the D.C. spring and their timeless message of beauty and friendship.

PURPLE POTATOES & CHERRY BLOSSOMS

WHAT *you'll need*

TOOLS: Bark wire
Straight wire (thinner gauge)
Bullion wire
Clippers
Wire cutters
Scissors
6-inch wired wood picks
4-inch water picks

MATERIALS:
1 18-inch grapevine wreath
1 roll of 1 ½-inch purple ribbon
90 mixed purple potatoes
1 pound of purple grapes
1 bunch of cherry branches
1 bunch fuchsia mokara orchids
7 small succulents

HOW-TO *instructions*   3 Expert   5-7 D

1   Wrap the bark wire around the wreath to create a loop for hanging.
2   Create a ribbon garland base layer using the ruched ribbon technique.
3   Using the straight wire, pierce the potatoes, stringing 5 together.
4   Lay the potato garland across the wreath, wrap the ends around and twist the wire together in the back.
5   Working in rows, continue adding potato garlands in this manner until the entire wreath is covered.
6   Wire small clusters of grapes to the wood picks and insert them throughout the wreath.
7   Add the succulents in the same manner using the wired wood picks.
8   Working in the same direction around the wreath, cut pieces of cherry blossom branches, insert in water picks, and angle them near the perimeter to create a spiral effect.
9   As a finishing touch, add small pieces of orchids (in water picks).

DESIGN *note*

Replace the cherry blossoms (and orchids) as needed;
the potatoes and succulents are a long-lasting design.

WHAT *you'll need*

TOOLS: Bark wire
1 roll of 1 ½-inch purple ribbon
Straight wire (thinner gauge)
Bullion wire
Clippers
Scissors
Wire cutters
4-inch water picks
6-inch wired wood picks

MATERIALS:
1 21-inch grapevine wreath
100 small purple potatoes
1 pound crabapples
2 bunches heather
1 bunch nandina foliage with berries

Across the mouth of Galway Bay, off the western coast of Ireland in the waters of North Atlantic sea, lies the rugged, windswept Aran Islands, a place that time has seemingly forgotten. Hauntingly beautiful, incredibly remote – accessible only by air or ferry – it's a landscape of jagged rocks, thatched roof houses, ancient forts and pastoral fields -- a place of raw, untamed natural splendor. Battered by storms and high winds, the islands' harsh weather sometimes lifts long enough to reveal glimpses of botanical life; the colors and forms make a strong impact set against the stark background of grey stone, sea and sky. Throughout the ages, rugged islanders have sought creative ways to defy nature's wrath, employing seaweed and sand to grow various crops and building low-slung stone walls in the fields for protection against the elements. This wreath of potatoes and heather with touches of nandina is inspired by the rocky landscape, colors and textures of the Aran Islands – a unique place of bleak beauty in the middle of the Wild Atlantic Way.

PURPLE POTATOES, CRABAPPLES & NANDINA

DESIGN *note*

Use faux crabapples from the craft store and substitute Italian ruscus for the nandina.

HOW-TO *instructions*

1   Wrap the bark wire around the wreath form to create a loop for hanging.
2   Create a purple ribbon base layer using the ruched ribbon technique.
3   Working side to side across the top of the wreath, attach the ruched ribbon garland to cover the top and sides of the wreath.
4   Using the straight wire, pierce the purple potatoes, stringing 5 together.
5   Lay the potato garland across the wreath, covering the sides and top, leaving some space in between each potato to let the ribbon show through.
6   Wrap the ends of the wire around the wreath, tying them securely in back.
7   Working in rows, continue adding individual strings of potatoes in this manner until the entire wreath is covered.
8   Using the straight wire, string 4 – 5 crabapples together, adding a bit extra wire to create longer garlands.
9   Lay the wire crabapple garlands over the top of the potatoes so that they float a bit above the surface, wrapping and tying the ends securely in back.
10   Add sprigs of heather using the wired wood picks.
11   Cut the nandina foliage into 6 – 8-inch pieces and wire them to the wood picks, inserting the foliage in and around the wreath, focusing on the inner and outer edges.

Located on the south bank of the Savannah River, situated between the Great Smokey Mountains and the Atlantic sea, Augusta, Georgia is the site of annual Masters Golf Tournament, which is always held during the first week of April when the azaleas typically bloom. The course is ringed by 30 colorful varieties and features the famous par 5 hole 13 -- named "Azalea" -- for the flower that is elegant (or gaudy) depending upon your point of view. This wreath is inspired by the signature Azalea cocktail that is featured at the event – a bright apple red and fuchsia fruity concoction that fans say requires a "mulligan" (do over) in golf lingo.

WHAT *you'll need*

TOOLS: Bark wire
Straight wire (thinner gauge)
Bullion wire
Clippers
Wire cutters
Scissors
6-inch wired wood picks
4-inch water picks

MATERIALS:
1 18-inch oval grapevine wreath
1 roll of 1 ½-inch apple red ribbon
Approximately 50 red apples
1 pint of red cherry tomatoes
1 bunch red hypericum berries
1 bunch hot pink azaleas
Several camellia blossoms

APPLE AZALEA

HOW-TO *instructions*

1 Wrap the bark wire around the wreath, doubling it, to create a loop for hanging.
2 Create a red ribbon base layer using the ruched ribbon technique.
3 Use the straight wire, pierce the apples, stringing 3 together to create a garland.
4 Place the apple string across the top of the wreath, wrapping the ends of the wire around the back and twisting them together. Clip the excess wire.
5 Wire the cherry tomatoes to the wood pick by stringing 3 together, wrapping the end of the wire to the wood pick.
6 Insert the cherry bundles evenly in and around the wreath.
7 Cut the hypericum berries into small pieces and insert them into the water picks, placing the berries across the top and sides of the wreath.
8 As a finishing touch, cut blossoms of camellia and pink azalea, insert them in water tubes and place them throughout the wreath so that the flowers float above the surface.

My favorite set of china is the vintage ironstone I discovered at a Virginia flea market several years ago. Called "Ivy Bower" and manufactured in England in the late 19th century, the pattern of birds and fruit in ivy is both sophisticated and charming. I especially love how the rich eggplant tones create a moody, vintage feeling, evoking a secret enchanted garden. Inspired by the vivid purple peppers and eggplants at the Old Town Farmers' Market, I created this wreath with an ivy bower border for a festive garden-themed dinner party.

PURPLE EGGPLANTS (IVY BOWER)

WHAT *you'll need*

TOOLS: Bark wire
Bullion wire
Paddle wire
Straight wire (thinner gauge)
Clippers
Wire cutters
Scissors
6-inch wired wood picks
4-inch water picks

MATERIALS:
1 18-inch grapevine wreath
1 roll of 1 ½-inch purple ribbon
5 purple bell peppers
30 small purple eggplants
3 stems blue/green hydrangea
1 bunch purple grapes (fresh or faux)
1 bunch green china berries
5 stems purple dendrobium orchid
Green trailing ivy

HOW-TO *instructions*

1. Wrap the bark wire around the wreath, doubling it, to create a loop for hanging.
2. Create a ribbon garland base layer using the ruched ribbon technique.
3. Attach bundles of grapes to the wreath with the paddle wire until the entire wreath is covered.
4. Using the straight wire, pierce the purple bell pepper and place it on the wreath, wrapping the wire around and twisting the ends in the back. Clip excess wire.
5. Continue adding the bell peppers in this manner, spacing them evenly.
6. Wire the eggplants by piercing with the straight wire, stringing 2 together.
7. Lay the eggplant string across the top of the wreath, wrapping the wire around and twisting the ends together in the back. Clip the excess wire.
8. Working in rows around the wreath, add the eggplant strings in the same manner to cover the entire wreath.
9. Insert sprigs of blue/green hydrangea (in water picks) in the wreath, placing them in and around the eggplant and bell peppers.
10. Wire sprigs of china berries with the wood picks and insert them in the wreath.
11. Cut small pieces of orchids, insert in water picks, and place the flowers so that they float above the other elements.
12. As a finishing touch, tuck strands of ivy in the wreath, focusing on the inside and outside edges.

For many years, brussels sprouts were maligned as the green vegetable every child (and many adults) hated to eat. But in the last few years, the lowly brussels sprout has surged to the forefront of culinary trends, landing squarely on the delicious list, a popular staple of trendy restaurants. In the kitchen they are ideally paired with bacon, but on the door I think variegated holly adds a lovely touch – the pointed shape and white-tipped leaf is the perfect counterpoint to the mini green cabbages, creating a festive holiday display in trendy monochrome shades of green and white.

BRUSSELS SPROUTS & HOLLY

WHAT *you'll need*

TOOLS: 1 18-inch oval straw wreath
Bark wire
1 roll 1 ½ moss green ribbon
6-inch wired wood picks
Straight wire (thinner gauge)
4-inch water picks

MATERIALS:
15 pounds of Brussels sprouts
1 bunch variegated holly
1 bunch red hypericum berry

HOW-TO *instructions*

1   Wrap the wreath with the bark wire to create a loop for hanging.
2   Prepare the base layer using the ruched ribbon technique, covering the front and sides of the wreath form in ribbon.
3   Insert the straight wire through the center of a Brussels sprouts, stringing 6 together.
4   Continue making garlands of Brussels sprouts.
5   Lay the garlands across the wreath, wrapping the wire ends around and securing them tightly in the back.
6   Working in even rows, continue adding the Brussels sprouts in this manner.
7   Cut the variegated holly into 6-inch pieces and wire them to the wood picks.
8   Insert the holly in and around the wreath, focusing on the outer and inside edges.
9   As a finishing touch, insert small pieces of hypericum berries into the water picks and insert evenly around the wreath.

For another version of a winter fruit and berry wreath, combine pomegranates, tangerines, dates and cranberries on a ribbon-covered base to create a "fruitcake" design: a celebration of the classic holiday treat. The cranberry lattice border adds an original touch, giving a light and lacy effect. This technique can be used to embellish a variety of different wreath designs. Here's how to create a festive fruitcake wreath with a cranberry lattice border.

FRUITCAKE & CRANBERRY LACE

WHAT *you'll need*

TOOLS: Bark wire
    Red bullion wire
    Straight wire (thinner gauge)
    Clippers
    Scissors
    Wire cutters

MATERIALS:
    1 18-inch grapevine wreath
    1 roll of 1 ½ inch red ribbon
    20 pomegranates
    3 bags of clementines
    (approximately 30 count)
    3 packages of fresh dates
    4 bags of fresh cranberries
    1 package of red pipe cleaners
    Green trailing ivy

HOW-TO *instructions*   3 Expert   5-7 D

1 Wrap the bark wire around the wreath to create as loop for hanging.
2 Create a ribbon base layer using the ruched ribbon technique.
3 Pierce the pomegranates with the straight wire, stringing 2 together.
4 Lay the pomegranates across the wreath, wrap the wire ends to the back, twisting tightly to secure. Clip the excess wire.
5 Working in rows, continue adding pomegranates in rows of 2.
6 Create garlands of clementines by stringing 3 together on a straight wire.
7 Wrap the wire ends of this garland around the wreath; secure in back.
8 Continue adding the clementine garlands until the entire wreath is covered.
9 Using the straight wire, string 4 – 5 dates together to create a garland.
10 Wrap the date garlands around the wreath, spacing them evenly among the clementines and pomegranates.
11 Working on the outside edge of the wreath, criss-cross the pipe cleaners to create an overlapping pattern forming a trellis effect.
12 Continue adding pipe cleaners, connecting the edges to create one border.
13 With the bullion wire, string the cranberries together, creating a garland a few inches in length.
14 Working in sections, wrap the cranberry garland around the pipe cleaner border, covering the entire surface.

Valentine's Day – that special day reserved for hearts and flowers, chocolate candy and expressions of love -- is celebrated in many cultures around the world, but perhaps South Korea has the most intriguing (and complicated) approach. On February 14, Valentine's Day honors men with women stepping up to give them chocolates as a sign of affection. A month later, on March 14, called "White Day" -- a tribute to women ensues when men are expected to reciprocate in kind with an array of chocolate treats. But on April 14, singles have their day – "Black Day" – when they dress in black clothing and eat black noodles – confirming their status as unlucky in love. This heart-shaped wreath of strawberries, berries and candy on a black door splits the difference and hedges bets: sending a hopeful message of love.

STRAWBERRY CANDY HEART

WHAT *you'll need*

TOOLS:
Bark wire
Bullion wire
Straight wire (thinner gauge)
Silver paddle wire
Clippers
Scissors
Wire cutters

MATERIALS:
1 16-inch metal (or grapevine) heart-shape wreath form
1 roll of fuchsia/red 1 ½-inch ribbon
2 pints of strawberries
1 bunch of red grapes
1 pint of cherry tomatoes
1 bunch of red pepper berry
1 bunch of berried ivy
1 bag of "x and o" Valentine's day candy
1 package of red pipe cleaners

HOW-TO *instructions*

1. Wrap the bark wire around the wreath to create a loop for hanging.
2. Create a ribbon base layer using the ruched ribbon technique.
3. Wrap the bark wire around the wreath to create a loop for hanging.
4. Using the straight wire, pierce the strawberries, stringing 3 together.
5. Working in rows around the wreath, wrap the strawberry garlands around the frame, twisting the wire ends together in back. Cut the excess wire.
6. Create strings of grape tomatoes in the same fashion, stringing 3 together.
7. Working in rows placed evenly around the wreath, attach the tomato garlands to the frame, securing the wire ends in back. Cut the excess wire.
8. Add a layer of grapes by stringing 3 together with the straight wire, wrapping these garlands in and around the base layers of strawberries and tomatoes, twisting the ends together in back.
9. Using the bullion wire, create garlands of berries by wiring bundles together.
10. Weave the garlands back and forth across the wreath in a zig zag pattern.
11. Add the ivy berries in the same manner, spacing the berries in and around.
12. Using the bullion wire, create garlands of candy by stringing 4 pieces together.
13. Wrap the candy garlands around the wreath so that they float above the form, securing the wire ends together in back.
14. Create a heart-shaped border by attaching pipe cleaners to the outer edge, folding the ends together in a heart-shaped motif, covering the entire wreath.

WHAT *you'll need*

TOOLS: Bark wire
Bind wire
Bullion wire
Straight wire
Clippers
Wire cutters
Scissors
6-inch wired wood picks

MATERIALS:
1 18-inch diamond form grapevine wreath
1 roll of 1 ½ inch green ribbon
12 bags of small limes
   (approximately 100 count)
3 pounds of green chile peppers
1 bunch of green china berries
1 bunch red hypericum berries
1 bunch cotoneaster foliage

Green fruits and vegetables with red berry accents creating a striking look during the holiday season and throughout the year. Use a grapevine (or wire) diamond-shaped wreath form to create this version of a lime and pepper wreath featuring a mix of materials from the market. The base is a layer of ruched moss ribbon with layers of wired limes and peppers finished with red and green berries and a touch of greenery.

SPICY LIME

HOW-TO *instructions*

1   Wrap the bark wire around the wreath to create a wreath for hanging.
2   Create a green ribbon base layer with the ruched ribbon technique.
3   Using the straight wire, pierce the limes, stringing 3 together.
4   Lay the lime garland across the wreath, spacing the limes evenly on the top and sides of the form.
5   Wrap the wire ends around and secure tightly in the back, clipping the excess wire.
6   Working in horizontal rows around the wreath, continue adding limes in this manner until the entire wreath is covered.
7   Using the straight wire, string 3 peppers together to create garlands.
8   Lay the pepper garland across the wreath and wrap the wire ends around to the back, twisting tightly to secure. Clip the excess wire.
9   Continue adding rows of peppers, spacing them in and around the limes .
10 Next, create small bundles of red and green berries using the wired wood picks.
11 Insert the wood picks in and around the wreath focusing on the edges.
12 As a finishing touch, create a narrow garland of cotoneaster with the bullion wire, wrapping sprigs of the greenery on to the bind wire to create a garland.
13 Attach the garland as a border, using the wired wood picks to secure it.

DESIGN *note*

Substitute hypericum berries for china berries depending upon seasonal availability.

Beyond the traditional array of red roses, a Valentine's Day heart can feature a variety of materials: apples, plums, berries, red bell peppers, candy – as long as they are in the requisite color palette of pink, red and plum. This charming wreath is made from garlands of cranberries and crabapples wrapped around a ribbon-covered heart-shaped frame bordered in ivy – a timeless symbol of love that helps to enhance the overall meaning and effect.

CRANBERRY & IVY HEART

WHAT *you'll need*

TOOLS: Bark wire
Bullion wire
Straight wire (thinner gauge)
Clippers
Scissors
Wire cutters
6-inch wire wood picks

MATERIALS:
1 roll of 1 ½-inch cranberry red ribbon
1 16-inch heart-shaped wreath form
4 bags of fresh cranberries
2 pounds of crabapples
1 bunch of rose hips
Green trailing ivy

HOW-TO *instructions*

 2 Medium 5-7 D

1 Wrap the bark wire around the wreath to create a loop for hanging.
2 Create a ribbon base layer using the ruched ribbon technique.
3 Using the straight wire, create garlands of cranberries, stringing 7 together.
4 Lay the cranberry garland across the wreath, wrap the wire ends around and secure tightly in the back. Clip the excess wire.
5 Working in tight rows around the wreath, continue adding garlands of cranberries until the entire wreath is covered.
6 Create garlands of crab apples, stringing 3 together.
7 Lay the crabapple garlands across the wreath, wrap the wire ends to the back and secure. Clip the excess wire.
8 Continue adding the crabapple garlands, spacing them evenly around the wreath.
9 Using the wood picks, wire small bundles of rose hips and insert them in the wreath so they float above the layer of cranberries and crabapples.
10 As a finishing touch, add a border of green trailing ivy, focusing on the interior and outside edges.

TIP

Add additional cranberries and crabapples at the rounded top part of the heart as well as at the bottom point to accentuate the heart shape.

This golden apple, pepper and tomato wreath reminds me of the magic golden light of summer when the trees and flowers are illuminated by the sunset's amber glow. For a fleeting moment, as the sun sinks slowly into the horizon, the colors seem to intensify, enveloping everything in a warm embrace -- creating a feeling of contentment, gratitude and grace. The delicate lantana blossoms add texture and lightness while a touch of greenery keeps the design feeling fresh.

HOW-TO *instructions*

1 Wrap the bark wire around the frame, doubling it, to create a loop for hanging.
2 Create a base of golden yellow ribbon garland using the ruched ribbon technique.
3 Using the straight wire, pierce the apples in the center, stringing 3 together.
4 Wrap the 3-apple garland across the front, securing the ends of the wire securely.
5 Continue adding the apple strings until the entire wreath is covered.
6 For the next layer, use the thinner straight wire to string 5 grape tomatoes, wrapping the garland across the wreath over the apples, tying the wire in the back.
7 Continue to add strings of grape tomatoes to cover the entire wreath.
8 Continue adding layers of texture with the yellow peppers: string 3 peppers together using the thinner wire and wrap the ends together, securing tightly.
9 Add the pepper strings to cover the wreath, spacing them about every 5 – 6-inches.
10 Insert sprigs of lantana in water tubes, adding them in and around the wreath.
11 As a finishing touch, wire pieces of ivy to the wire wood picks to create a border inside and outside the wreath.

| GOLDEN APPLE

WHAT *you'll need*

TOOLS: 1 18-inch grapevine wreath
Bark wire
Clippers
Wire cutters
6-inch wired wood picks
4-inch water picks
Straight wire (heavier gauge)
Straight wire (lighter gauge)
Bullion wire

MATERIALS:
1 roll of 1 ½-inch yellow ribbon
8 bags of golden apples
   (add approximately 48 count)
2 pints of yellow grape tomatoes
3 bags of small yellow peppers
Sprigs of lantana blooms
Green trailing ivy

DESIGN *note*

Substitute yellow orchids or another summer flower for the lantana.

For this version of the apple wreath, I used "Cripps Pink" apples from Washington State for a slightly more subtle color and effect. The gentle pink tone works well in many seasons, adding a touch of lightness and warmth, and blends nicely with various styles of exterior landscapes and architectural decor. Here, I've created a summery apple wreath with "pinky flair" hypericum berries arranged on a base of ivy and evergreens, displayed on a grape arbor. Although I like the simplicity and form of the apples and berries just by themselves, a touch of scented jasmine vine would be a perfect addition.

WHAT *you'll need*

TOOLS: Bark wire
Straight wire (thinner gauge)
Paddle wire
Clippers
Wire cutters
4-inch water picks (optional)

MATERIALS:
1 18-inch grapevine wreath
1 roll of 1 ½-inch moss green ribbon
85 – 95 pink apples
1 bunch of red hypericum berries
Optional: jasmine vine

PINK APPLES & BERRIES

HOW-TO *instructions* 2 Medium 5-7 D

1 Wrap the wreath with bark wire to create a loop for hanging.
2 Create a base layer of moss green ribbon using the ruched ribbon technique.
3 Using the straight wire, pierce the apples, stringing 3 together, placing the garland across the top of the wreath.
4 Wrap the wire ends around the wreath, securing them tightly in the back. Clip the excess wire.
5 Working in rows, continue adding apple garlands in this manner until the entire wreath form is covered.
6 Cut the hypericum berries into small pieces, insert them in water tubes and place in and around the apples throughout the wreath.
7 As an optional finishing touch, insert individual jasmine vines into the water picks, positioning them evenly around the wreath.

DESIGN *note*

Add orchid blossoms and/or sweet pea vines in rosy tones as another optional finishing touch.

Although I generally start my designs with a basic idea of color and composition, I enjoy leaving things open ended so I can improvise on the spot. Often my inspiration happens on a casual stroll through the farmers' market or when I'm at the local grocery store pushing an empty cart. Just as a chef might survey the produce aisle for appealing items to include in a recipe, I scan the weekly offerings looking for inspiring colors and shapes that will enhance my designs. I'm often drawn to experimental combinations, things I haven't seen or tried before. This orange carrot and pepper combination is one of those designs – and could probably be turned into an interesting roasted carrot hot sauce, too.

WHAT *you'll need*

TOOLS: Bark wire
Bullion wire
Paddle wire
6-inch wired wood picks
Straight wire (thinner gauge)

MATERIALS:
1 18-inch straw wreath
6 bags of mini carrots
1 ½ lbs. habanero peppers
2 bunches evergreen/fir tips
1 bunch berried ivy

DESIGN *note*

Carrots will become lighter after a couple of days. Spray with a mixture of acrylic floor wax to increase longevity.

TIP

When working with hot peppers, it's a good idea to wear gloves to protect skin and eyes from irritation.

CARROTS & PEPPERS

HOW-TO *instructions*   2 Medium   5-7 D

1   Wrap the bark wire around the straw frame to create a loop for hanging.

2   Prepare the base of the wreath by cutting and tying the fir tips into small bundles using the bullion wire.

3   Add the fir bundles to the wreath frame by wrapping the bundles. at the base with paddle wire, working in horizontal rows across the frame.

4   Continue adding rows of fir, wrapping the bundles tightly to the wreath until the entire surface is covered.

5   Using the straight wire, pierce through the middle of the carrot, stringing 7 on each wire.

6   Wrap the carrot garland across the top of the wreath frame, tying the wires tightly together in back.

7   Working around the frame in rows, continue adding strings of carrots to the base until the entire wreath is covered.

8   Using the paddle wire, pierce the habanero peppers, stringing 5 together to make a garland.

9   Working in rows, wrap the habanero pepper garlands across the wreath, interspersing them in and around the carrots, all the way around the wreath.

In the summer time, I often blend fruits, flowers, vegetables and trailing vines from the farmers' market in my wreath designs – seasonal elements that combine to evoke the lushness and bounty of summer. One of the great benefits of living in the little historic village of Old Town Alexandria, Virginia is the weekly Saturday farmers' market that is literally a stone's throw from my front door. The Farmers' Market was founded by George Washington in 1753 and is the oldest continuously operating market in the United States. The market is a delightful place throughout the year, but is especially charming in summer. That's when the town square is awash in color and character with stall after stall of flowers, plants, fruits and vegetables from local fields and farms. It bustles on Saturday morning with locals and visitors alike, with the cream of the market's bounty always going to the early birds who rouse at dawn for the best first picks. For this wreath, I was inspired by the delicate size, round shape and bright golden color of the small yellow tomatoes I found at the market. I gathered up a few pints and headed back to my garden where I snipped some ivy and ferns to complement a moss-covered frame. Here is how the piece came together.

YELLOW TOMATO & IVY

WHAT *you'll need*

TOOLS: Barked wire
1 bag of green sheet moss
Straight wire (thinner gauge)
Bullion wire
6-inch wired wood picks
Paddle wire
Wire cutters

MATERIALS:
18-inch straw wreath form
10 – 12 pints of yellow grape tomatoes
Garden ivy

HOW-TO *instructions*

1 Wrap the bark wire around the straw form, creating a loop for hanging.
2 Attach the sheet moss to the front of the wreath, wrapping the moss with paddle wire to bind it securely to the frame.
3 Using the straight wire, create strings of 7 yellow tomatoes.
4 Wrap the strings across the moss-covered frame, tying them securely in the back. Cut excess wire with the wire cutters.
5 Add wired tomato strings in rows, working evenly until the entire frame is covered.
6 Cut the ivy into 6 – 8-inch pieces, wiring the end to the wood pick.
7 Insert the ivy pieces into the frame at intervals to create a natural border with flowing tendrils.

WHAT *you'll need*

TOOLS: Bark wire
Straight wire (thinner gauge)
Bullion wire
6-inch wired wood picks
4-inch water picks

MATERIALS:
1 18-inch grapevine wreath
1 roll of 2-inch wired edge gold ribbon
20 peaches
40 apricots
2 pints of yellow cherry tomatoes
1 bunch of bittersweet vines
Sprigs of yellow lantana blossoms

As a child, I remember spending long hours in my grandfather's library, a cozy and welcoming space with book-lined walls and a blazing hearth. While he read sophisticated historical novels and biographies, I perused a children's section that included a fairly sizable collection of literary classics and Dr. Seuss, as well as mysteries, fairy tales and quirky vintage books. One of my favorite corners contained the flower and gardening books, including several Victorian tomes on the symbolic meaning of flowers. I still remember one particular book of rhyming verse that issued dire warnings about plants with scary names – deadly nightshade, devil's claw, witch hazel, ghost plants – cautioning that their alluring beauty disguises horrible deadly consequences if ingested. The compelling prose definitely made an impression on me. Although it looks good enough to eat, this wreath of tangled brambles and bittersweet vine (also known as deadly nightshade or poisonberry) mixed with peaches and apricots in golden hues is designed only for visual enjoyment and delight.

PEACHES, APRICOTS & BITTERSWEET

HOW-TO *instructions*

1 Craft a ribbon base layer with the ruched ribbon technique.
2 Wrap the bark wire around the wreath to create a loop for hanging.
3 Using the straight wire, pierce the peaches close to the center, stringing 2 together.
4 Lay the peach garland across the top of the wreath, wrap the wire ends around, and secure together in back. Cut the excess wire.
5 Working in rows around the wreath, add peach garlands until the entire form is evenly covered.
6 Create garlands of apricots in the same manner, stringing 3 together.
7 Working in rows around the wreath, add garlands of apricots, placing them in between the peaches, covering the top and sides of the wreath.
8 Using the straight wire, create garlands of yellow tomatoes, stringing 4 together.
9 Add the tomato garlands, wrapping them evenly across the wreath in rows, filling in gaps, creating additional texture.
10 Cut the bittersweet vine into various lengths and wire the ends using wood picks.
11 Tuck the berries in and around, placing longer vines on the outside edges.
12 Add sprigs of lantana by placing water-filled picks at intervals around the form so that the flowers float above the fruit.

DESIGN *note*

Use firm, unripened peaches and apricots for the best result.

WHAT *you'll need*

TOOLS:
- Bark wire
- Bullion wire
- Paddle wire
- Straight wire (thinner gauge)
- Clippers
- Wire cutters
- Scissors
- 4-inch wired wood picks

MATERIALS:
- 1 15-inch straw wreath
- 40 tangerines
- 8 pounds of red fingerling potatoes
- 15 apricots
- Small pale pink shiny ornaments
- Green ivy

During the reign of King Louis XIV who lived from 1638-1715, Versailles was a perfume-filled floral foam full of flowers and rose petal bowls, blooming jasmine and orange blossom topiaries, and probably fairly pungent odors, too. The Sun King was apparently so frightened of bathing that he reportedly took only 3 baths during his entire lifetime. As a result, royal perfumers worked overtime to mask any noxious orders, spraying furniture, clothing and even visitors to Versailles with sweet-smelling fragrant scents. The King personally favored strong and spicy scents of wood, nutmeg, cloves and rosewater but encouraged his perfumers to conjure up new and intricate combinations to waft through the palace grounds. The French perfume industry reached its zenith during his reign. Later, in the mid-18th century, Marie Antoinette (who was married to Louis XVI) favored flowery concoctions of tuberose, jasmine, orange and rose blossoms that were specifically designed to match her personality. For this wintertime iteration of the tangerine wreath, I incorporated apricots, potatoes and a few pink baubles to create a translucent effect for a light-catching window display. The tangerines provide a fresh and tangy scent while the apricots add a sweet mellow note. Interior window wreaths are an excellent way to bring color and texture indoors during the holiday season and throughout the long winter months – as well as infuse the air with pleasant scents in the tradition of Versailles.

ORANGES, APRICOTS, POTATOES "WINTER FRUITS"

HOW-TO *instructions*

1 Wrap sprigs of ivy around the straw form using the paddle wire to create a light base layer.

2 Wrap the bark wire around the wreath to create a loop for hanging.

3 Pierce the tangerines with the straight wire, stringing 3 together.

4 Lay the tangerine garlands across the wreath, wrapping ends around, twisting the wire ends together in the back.

5 Continue adding tangerines in this manner until the entire wreath is covered.

6 Pierce the apricots with the straight wire close to the center and wire onto the wreath, spacing them evenly.

7 Create garlands of potatoes with the straight wire, stringing 3 together.

8 Wrap the garlands around the wreath, weaving the potatoes in and around the tangerines and apricots.

9 Insert the ornaments using the wood picks, occasionally clustering two together.

10 As a finishing touch, add sprigs of ivy, focusing on the interior and outside edges.

On the way to the San Juan Islands, the idyllic archipelago off the coast of Washington state, the scenery along the highway is unbelievably spectacular. As the road winds through evergreen forests and rugged hills, the vast expanse of Puget Sound is always visible below, with sunlight sparkling off the waters, casting a summer spell. I remember a time we stopped for dinner at a quirky country inn where the flavor du jour was Rainier cherries – that quintessential fruit of the Northwest summer – paired with oranges in every course: in home-made scones, a salmon sauce, the field greens salad and dessert – a delicious cherry and orange liqueur pie. With an orange and cherry Campari cocktail as the quintessential "cherry on top," we were reminded that life indeed is like a bowl of cherries. This wreath of cherries and oranges, accented by scented geranium, reminds me of that sentiment and that special summer day.

ORANGES, CHERRIES & GERANIUM

WHAT *you'll need*

TOOLS:
Bark wire
Bullion wire
Clippers
Wire cutters
Scissors
6-inch wired wood picks
4-inch water picks

MATERIALS:
1 18-inch grapevine wreath
1 roll of 1 ½-inch citrus yellow or orange ribbon
100 mandarin oranges
2 pints of golden cherries
1 bunch of scented geranium foliage
sprigs of lantana

HOW-TO *instructions*   2 Medium   5-7 D

1 Wrap the bark wire around the wreath, doubling it, to create a loop for hanging.
2 Create a ribbon garland base using the ruched ribbon technique.
3 Using the straight wire, pierce the orange and string 4 together.
4 Wrap the wire ends around and twist them together in the back to secure.
5 Working in rows, add the orange garlands until the wreath is covered.
6 Using the straight wire, pierce a golden cherry with the straight wire, stringing 5 together.
7 Lay the cherry garland across the top of the wreath, spacing the cherries evenly to cover the entire surface.
8 Wrap the wire ends around and twist together in the back. Clip the excess wire.
9 Working in rows, add the cherry garlands around the wreath.
10 Insert sprigs of geranium foliage into the water tubes and place them on the wreath, focusing on the inside and outside edges.
11 As a finishing touch, insert lantana blossoms (in water tubes) so that the flowers float slightly above the fruit.

This orange wreath, "La Couronne d'Orange," is inspired by the L'Orangerie at Versailles, an immense 17th century gallery that houses a vast collection of orange and lemon topiaries, oleander, palm and pomegranate trees. King Louis XIV loved orange trees for their perfume and sweet blooms and brought the citrus trees indoors, often displaying them in silver urns. For a mid-winter fête with a Versailles theme, this orange wreath welcomes guests with its namesake cheery color and lovely scent. The festive orange theme continues inside where the table is set with Orange Paris porcelain and bouquets of orange tulips and roses, while the menu includes coordinating food and drink – and guests are dressed to match.

ORANGE PEPPER

WHAT *you'll need*

HOW-TO *instructions*

TOOLS: Bark wire
Bullion wire
Paddle wire
Straight wire
6-inch wire wood picks

MATERIALS:
1 16-inch straw wreath frame
1 roll of 1 ½-inch orange ribbon
50 mandarin oranges
2 pounds of habanero peppers
1 bunch Italian ruscus

1   Wrap the bark wire around the frame to create a loop for hanging.
2   Make the ribbon base layer by crafting a ruched ribbon garland.
3   Secure the ribbon garland to the front of the frame, wrapping it back and forth, using the paddle wire to tie the ends.
4   Using the straight wire, pierce the oranges, string 4 together.
5   Wrap the orange garland strings across the front of the wreath, securing the wire in back. Clip the excess wire.
6   Working in rows, continue adding the oranges until the wreath is covered.
7   Create similar garlands of the habenara peppers using the paddle wire, stringing 5 – 6 together.
8   Wrap the habanero pepper garlands across the top of the oranges, securing the wire in back. Clip the excess wire.
9   Continue adding the habanero peppers, working in rows around the wreath.
10 As a finishing touch, insert pieces of Italian ruscus into the wreath frame using the wired wood picks.

WHAT *you'll need*

TOOLS: Bark wire
Bullion wire
Straight wire (thinner gauge)
Clippers
Wire cutters
Scissors
6-inch wired wood picks
4-inch water picks

MATERIALS: (for each wreath):
1 14-inch square wire frame wreath
1 roll of 1 ½-inch lemon yellow ribbon
45 lemons
1 pint yellow grape tomatoes
2 bunches mint
Green trailing ivy

As a child, lemon yellow – bright, bold sunny citrus yellow -- was my favorite color. So at age 10, when I received permission to redecorate my room, I chose yellow as the basis of my décor scheme: the paint for my antique bedroom set (!), for all of the rugs and bedding, and for the ruffled gingham curtains in the room. My grandmother helped me with the sewing projects, including the box pleat dust ruffle and smocked pillows, while I painted the furniture myself (which resulted in a few too many drips and cat hairs in the mix). The *piece de resistance* of my décor was an antique yellow patchwork quilt in a "double wedding ring" motif, handmade by my great-grandmother when she was 103 years old. All in all, it was incredibly exciting and rewarding to see my vision come together – a room that exuded sunshine and happiness even on the dreariest of northwest gray days. These fresh lemon and mint interior wreaths, displayed in the windows of my (yellow) front parlor so that they catch and reflect the intense morning light, remind of the sunny, inspiring spirit of my childhood room.

LEMON MINT (INTERIOR WREATHS)

HOW-TO *instructions*

1 Wrap the bark wire around the wreath to create a loop for hanging.
2 Create a ribbon garland for the base using the ruched ribbon technique.
3 Using the straight wire, pierce a lemon, stringing two together.
4 Lay the lemon garland across the wreath, wrap the wire ends around and twist together in the back. Clip the excess wire.
5 Working in rows, continue to add lemon strings in this manner until the entire wreath is covered.
6 Next, create strings of yellow grape tomatoes by stringing 3 together.
7 Lay the tomato strings across the top of the wreath, wrap the wire ends around and twist together in back to secure. Clip the excess wire.
8 Insert sprigs of mint into the water tubes and place in and around the lemons throughout the wreath.
9 As a finishing touch, add a piece of trailing ivy to cover the bark wire.

In northern Virginia along the Potomac River near George Washington's River Farm, summer sometimes skips into autumn at a fairly quick clip. One day, the trees are lush and green and the air is balmy but with just a slight hint of winter chill. And then seemingly overnight, usually in early October, nature flips a switch, and the backdrop changes from vivid summer to muted fall full of amber colors and golden light. For this autumn take on the orange wreath, I added fall elements and textures in a mix of bright and burnished hues.

ORANGES, ROSEHIPS & YELLOW ORCHIDS

WHAT *you'll need*

TOOLS: Bark wire
Bullion wire
Straight wire (thinner gauge)
Clippers
Wire cutters
Scissors
4-inch water picks
6-inch wired wood picks

MATERIALS:
1 18-inch diamond form grapevine wreath
1 ½-inch moss green ribbon
60 oranges
1 brunch orange coxcomb
1 bunch yellow oncidium orchid
1 bunch rosehips
Green ivy

HOW-TO *instructions*   2 Medium   5-7 D

1 Wrap the bark wire around the frame to create a loop for hanging.
2 Create a ribbon base layer using the ruched ribbon technique.
3 Pierce the oranges with the straight wire, stringing 3 together.
4 Lay the orange garlands across the wreath, wrap around and twist the ends together in the back. Cut the excess wire.
5 Insert short stems of coxcomb in water picks and place evenly around the wreath.
6 Attach sprigs of rosehips to the wood picks and insert so that they float above the wreath.
7 Cut the oncidium orchids into smaller pieces; insert in water tubes and place in and around the wreath, focusing on the interior and outside edges.
8 Using the wood picks, add the ivy as a finishing touch.

This orange peel design features a different kind of fruit wreath-making technique: instead of wiring whole oranges to the frame, the oranges are carved into wedges and pinned on to the form to create an intricate patterned design. Simple in form and use of materials, this carved fish-scale orange wreath is perfect on a classical or contemporary façade.

HOW-TO *instructions*

1 Wrap the bark wire around the wreath to create a loop for hanging.
2 Cut the oranges into quarters and remove the fruit, leaving the peel, creating wedges.
3 Working from left to right in rows across the wreath, pin the peels onto the wreath, inserting a u-pin at the base of each wedge.
4 Continue adding overlapping rows of orange peel wedges to cover the entire wreath, placing the peels to hide the u-pins.
5 Create narrow garlands of ivy using the bind wire as the base and paddle wire to add ivy, wrapping sprigs around the bindwire.
6 Pin the garlands to the interior and outside edges to create a border.

| ORANGE PEEL

WHAT *you'll need*

TOOLS: Bark wire
Bind wire
Paddle wire
Knife
u-pins
Bullion wire
MATERIALS:
1 25-inch straw wreath
60 – 65 oranges
Green ivy

DESIGN *note*

Although this is not an especially long-lasting wreath, it packs a punch as a party design and provides fresh-squeezed orange juice to boot!

WHAT *you'll need*

TOOLS: Bark wire
Bullion wire
Straight wire (thinner gauge)
Clippers
Wire cutters
Scissors
6-inch wired wood picks

MATERIALS:

1 18-inch grapevine wreath
1 roll of 1 ½-inch emerald green ribbon
100 limes
1 bunch seasonal red berries
(e.g., ilex, holly or hypericum)
1 bunch green hypericum berries
1 bunch of green or variegated holly

In the 18th century, Gadsby's Tavern in Alexandria, Virginia was a popular gathering place for our fledgling nation's political elite where patrons debated important issues of the day over a frothy tankard of ale. Among his numerous innovations and contributions to our country, George Washington is also known for introducing rum punch to America and his favorite local watering hole – a citrusy sweet, yet robust concoction reportedly discovered on his trip to Barbados in 1751. The General apparently returned to Virginia with a stockpile of rum, later distilling it at Mount Vernon. Today, Gadsby's Tavern celebrates George Washington – and this Caribbean elixir -- with an annual rum punch recipe contest. This lime wreath, hanging a stone's throw away from Gadsby's Tavern, pays homage to this interesting colonial tradition.

| LIMES, BERRIES & HOLLY

HOW-TO *instructions*

1   Wrap the bark wire around the wreath, doubling it, to create a loop for hanging.
2   Create a base layer of emerald green ribbon using the ruched ribbon technique.
3   With the straight wire, string 4 limes together, laying the lime garland across the wreath.
4   Wrap the wire ends to the back, twisting them together to secure tightly. Clip the excess wire.
5   Working in rows, continue adding garlands of limes in this manner until the entire wreath is covered.
6   Cut sprigs of red berries and wire them to the wood picks.
7   Working side to side, insert the red and green berries in and around the wreath to cover the entire surface.
8   As a finishing touch, add sprigs of green holly using the wired wood picks.

DESIGN *note*

Although this wreath has universal seasonal appeal, the colors are most striking on a white or red door.

In ancient mythology, the bee was thought to be a sacred insect with mystical qualities, a symbol of community, cooperation and personal potential. In the early 18th century, Napoleon Bonaparte, Emperor of France, was so taken with the bee's symbolism and tenacious nature that he adopted the honey bee as an emblem that defined his power and prestige. Of all the bees, the notorious Queen Bee is perhaps the source of the most awe-inspiring mystique. Dominant and controlling of all the drones in the hive, she eliminates potential female rivals with a swift and deadly strike. The Queen Bee's power is tenuous, however; the same drones that cater to her can deliver a lethal blow at any point, ending her reign in an abrupt and undignified fashion. This wreath, featuring a large Queen Bee made of lemons, coffee bean stripes and dried mushroom wings is surrounded by the worker bees that cater to her until when they don't.

QUEEN BEE

WHAT *you'll need*

TOOLS: Bark wire
Straight wire (thinner gauge)
Bullion wire
Tooth picks
24 karat gold spray paint
Gold berries
Hot glue
Hot glue gun
4-inch water picks

MATERIALS:
1 18-inch grapevine wreath
Brown craft paper (or grocery bags)
21 lemons
1 pound of coffee beans
1 yellow bell pepper
13 small yellow squash
1 bunch gold branches
Dried mushrooms
Yellow begonia
Coleus foliage

HOW-TO *instructions*

1 Wrap the bark wire around the wreath to create a loop for hanging.
2 Create a textured "honeycomb" base layer by folding the craft paper into " paper catchers," gluing them in rows around the wreath.
3 Spray the paper-covered wreath with gold spray.
4 Hot glue bands of coffee around all of the lemons to resemble bumble bees. Spray tooth picks with gold point to create antenna, top with gold berries, and insert in the lemons.
5 Create a "queen bee" with the yellow pepper, adding coffee stripes and a lemon head. Add gold toothpicks to create antenna, top with gold berries.
6 Insert dried mushrooms (available from floral suppliers) into the yellow pepper to create wings.
7 Using the straight wire, attach the lemons to the frame working in rows around the wreath, wrapping the wire ends to the back, twisting to secure. Cut the excess wire.
8 Create a garland of gold branches with the bullion wire; attach to the outside edge of the wreath.
9 Using the water picks, insert the begonia and coleus in and around the wreath.

If I am lucky enough to be at the Parisian flower market in the spring, I make a beeline for the stall with the French violets. Petite and chic, the charming little bouquets of purple fragrant blooms always stand out among the sea of inspiring floral displays, beckoning me with their beguiling scent and incomparable beauty. Interestingly, it was Napoleon III who solidified the place of the humble violet as a symbol of loyalty and perseverance – a personal emblem with sentimental meaning. Upon his defeat in 1814, he famously vowed that just like the violets that bloom in the Chateau Fontainebleau gardens, he would return within a year. Although his vision of victory (and violets) didn't quite pan out according to plan, Napoleon remained attached to the sweet violet, elevating it to his signature bloom. This wreath of violets mixed with spring flowers is inspired by the enduring symbolism and simple beauty of the humble purple violet in the French Empire period tradition.

SWEET VIOLETS

WHAT *you'll need*

TOOLS:
1 length of heavy wire
   (for the wreath frame)
Bark wire
Black binding wire
Green paddle wire
Clippers
Wire cutters
Spray bottle of water

MATERIALS:
1 bag of green sheet moss
1 large bunch of green bush ivy
2 bunches of violets
5 stems of purple hydrangea
3 stems hot pink hydrangea
1 bunch of purple campula
2 bunches of green hellebores
1 bunch of orange spray roses
1 bunch pink mini carnations

HOW-TO *instructions*

1 Cut the wire to the length of the wreath, extending it several-inches for binding.
2 Wrap the wire into a circle so that the ends overlap and bind together with the black binding wire.
3 Using the paddle wire, add moss to the wire form, wrapping continuously around the frame.
4 Wrap bark wire around the wreath to create a loop for hanging.
5 Spray the moss wreath form with water.
6 Next, using the paddle wire, add small bundles of green ivy to create a light base layer.
7 Prepare the flowers by cutting them into small 2-3-inch pieces.
8 Working left to right in rows around the wreath, add the flowers in small bunches to the form, using the paddle wire.
9 As a finishing touch, push longer stems of hellebores and campanula in the wreath around the edges to resemble butterflies.

DESIGN *note*

This wreath will last 3 – 4 days in cool weather. Keep it watered and lightly misted to extend its lifespan. Tip: spray the inside of a plastic bag with water and cover the wreath to keep it fresh for a special occasion.

As a toddler, I apparently had strong sartorial instincts. My mom recounts the story of dressing me in a hot pink dress with a red sweater before pre-school one day. After assessing the choices she made, I apparently stomped my foot, crossed my arms and said with definitive conviction: "I won't wear that – pink and red don't go together!" While I don't remember the origin of my strong feelings about this particular color combination, I do know that my opinions about the pairing have mellowed over the years. The turning point was when I started going to Paris and observed this bold color scheme in use everywhere – in fashion, interior décor, gardens – and even decorating the restrooms at Charles De Gaulle international airport. The combination of hot pink and red has definitely grown on me as a color palette and is the source of inspiration for this bold wreath: a combination of vivid red grape tomatoes and dendrobium orchids in a bright fuchsia hue.

RED TOMATO & FUCHSIA ORCHID

WHAT *you'll need*

TOOLS: Bark wire
Bullion wire
Straight wire (thinner gauge)
½-inch floral tape
6-inch wired wood picks
4-inch water picks

MATERIALS:
1 18-inch straw wreath form
1 roll of 1 ½ inch fuchsia ribbon
12 1 pint boxes of mini grape tomatoes
1 bunch of fuchsia dendrobium orchids

HOW-TO *instructions*

1 Wrap the bark wire around the straw frame to create a loop for hanging.
2 Create a ribbon garland as the base layer using the ruched ribbon technique.
3 Using the straight wire, pierce the tomatoes, stringing 7 together.
4 Position the tomato garland evenly over the top and sides of the ruched ribbon base, tying and securing the wire in the back. Clip the excess wire.
5 Working in rows, add the strings of red tomatoes in this manner until the entire frame is covered.
6 Cut the dendrobium orchids into 3 – 4-inch pieces, leaving a 2-inch stem; insert them in water tubes.
7 Attach the water tubes to the wired wood picks by wrapping them with floral tape.
8 Create approximately 2 dozen wired orchids.
9 Add the orchids to the wreath by placing the wood pick in the frame, positioning the orchid on both the inner and outer edges, creating a balanced presentation.

One of the more interesting materials that is unique to fall is a plant called "pumpkin trees" or "pumpkins on a stick." The plant is actually an ornamental eggplant variety that grows on tall stalks, producing miniature orange fruits that resemble pumpkins. Decorative and long-lasting, the pumpkin tree fruits are a popular element for seasonal floral arrangements; I think they also make wonderful wreaths.

PUMPKIN PATCH

WHAT *you'll need*

TOOLS: Bark wire
Bullion wire
Straight wire (thinner gauge)
Clippers
Wire cutters
Scissors
6-inch wired wood picks

MATERIALS:
1 18-inch grapevine wreath
1 roll of 1 ½-inch moss green ribbon
8 stems of "pumpkin trees"
1 bunch rose hips
Berried green ivy

HOW-TO *instructions*

1 Wrap the bark wire around the wreath to create a loop for hanging.
2 Create a moss green base layer using the ruched ribbon technique.
3 Cut the eggplant "pumpkins" and string 4 together using the straight wire.
4 Lay the pumpkin garland across the wreath, wrap the wire around, twisting the ends together in back. Cut the excess wire.
5 Working in rows, continue adding pumpkins in this manner until the entire wreath is covered.
6 Wire small pieces of rose hips to the wood picks and place them throughout the wreath focusing on the interior and outside edges.
7 As a finishing touch, add sprigs of berried ivy using the wood picks to create a border.

DESIGN *note*

This is a long-lasting wreath – the "pumpkins" and rose hips dry well in cool weather.

WHAT *you'll need*

TOOLS: Bark wire
Bullion wire
Straight wire (thinner gauge)
6-inch wired wood picks
4-inch water picks

MATERIALS:

1 18-inch grapevine wreath
1 roll of 1 ½-inch green ribbon
30 small green and white squashes/
   pumpkins (fresh or faux)
3 pounds of small fingerling potatoes
3 pounds of small zucchini/okra
40 small green apples
   (or small green peppers)
1 bunch white hyacinth
Dogwood branches
Green ivy

As a tribute to Thomas Jefferson who grew American dogwoods on his beloved Monticello estate, Virginia lawmakers decreed that the elegant tree with the snow white blossoms would be the official state tree and flower in 1918. It's easy to see why. With a distinctive 4-petal bract and bright green center, the dogwood is a unique and iconic emblem of the Virginia spring. When composing wreaths or flower arrangements, I like to use dogwood as the finishing touch – inserting it last so it floats above the design like the butterfly it resembles. Here, I've used a fresh palette of green and white squash, okra, and ivy as the base for displaying the dogwood blossoms.

GREEN SQUASH, DOGWOOD & ZUCCHINI

HOW-TO *instructions* (2 Medium) 5-7 D

1 Wrap the bark wire around the wreath to create a loop for hanging.
2 Create a base layer of green ribbon using the ruched ribbon technique.
3 Using the straight wire, pierce the squash, stringing 3 together, alternating colors and shapes.
4 Lay the squash garland across the top of the wreath, wrapping the ends around and securing them together in the back. Cut the excess wire.
5 Continue attaching squash to the wreath in this manner, working in rows around the wreath.
6 Using the straight wire, create potato garlands, stringing 4 together.
7 Wrap the potato garlands over the top of the wreath, in and around the squash. Tie the wire ends together in back. Cut the excess wire.
8 Next, create zucchini and apple garlands with the straight wire, stringing 3 together.
9 Place the garlands across the wreath and, working in rows, continue adding these elements, spacing them over and around the squash.
10 As a finishing touch, cut pieces of dogwood blossoms, insert them in water picks and place the flowers in and around the wreath.

WHAT *you'll need*

TOOLS: Bullion wire
Bark wire
Wire cutters
Scissors
Glue gun
Glue sticks
4-inch water picks

MATERIALS:
1 18-inch straw wreath
2 rolls of 4 – 6-inch burlap wired
edge ribbon
15 pounds of mixed shells of various sizes
10 small starfish (from the craft store)
3 stems of orange mokara orchid
1 bunch of white flowers (e.g., azalea,
alstromeria, etc.)

During the lazy summer months, the ocean beckons with shining sand and sparkling sea, the promise of sun, gentle breezes and the mesmerizing sound of rolling waves crashing on the shore. As the frothy white caps dance and roll on their journey back out to sea, leaving scores of pretty shells in their wake, my collector's impulse takes over and I'm always inspired to gather up this beautiful bounty of the sea. Back home, the souvenirs are reminders of a magical time and place, providing a source of endless creative inspiration. This wreath of shells and coral orchids, with seagrass and summery white blooms, evokes the timeless allure of summers at the shore.

| CORAL REEF

HOW-TO *instructions*

1 Wrap the wreath form with the bark wire, doubling it, to create a loop for hanging.
2 Using the burlap ribbon and bullion wire, create a base layer of 4-inch ruched ribbon loops.
3 Working side to side across the wreath, tie the ruched ribbon garland to the wreath form, covering the sides and top of the wreath.
4 Glue the shells to the burlap, mixing in various shapes and sizes to create a textured tapestry of shells, covering the sides and top of the wreath.
5 Cut the orange orchid stems into several small pieces, insert in water picks.
6 Add the orchids to the outside edge of the wreath, focusing on the perimeter so that the flowers resemble touches of coral.
7 Continue adding small touches of white flowers using the same method, placing these water picks in and around the wreath in decorative clusters.

DESIGN *note*

You can purchase a wide variety
of shells at the craft store
to augment your personal collection
from the sea shore.

On the beautiful island of Faial in the Azores archipelago off the coast of Portugal, the hydrangea bloom in abundant profusion, along the roadsides, creating hedgerows, in gardens and throughout the island. Named the "blue island" by Portugese poet Raul Brandao in honor of its most notable floral feature, Faial is especially charming in summer, when the hydrangeas are in full bloom. From the air, the views are astounding: a patchwork grid of blue outlining lush pastures and fields where peaceful sheep and cattle roam. The heavenly blue hydrangeas leave a lasting impression, lingering as the indelible emblem of this idyllic paradise. The blue hydrangea wreath is inspired by the colors, scents and incredible natural beauty of Faial – the "blue" Island of the Azores.

| BLUE HYDRANGEA

WHAT *you'll need*

TOOLS: Bark wire
Clippers
Wire cutters

MATERIALS:
1 21-inch floral foam wreath
10 stems white hydrangea
10 stems blue hydrangea
3 bunches of blue iris
10 purple lantana blossoms
2 bunches of green trailing ivy

HOW-TO *instructions*

1 Wrap the floral foam wreath form with bark wire to create a loop for hanging.
2 Soak the floral foam form in water, making sure the wreath is fully saturated.
3 Cut the heads of the white hydrangea into smaller pieces and insert them around the sides and top of the wreath form, working in drifts, creating a ribbon of hydrangea around the wreath.
4 Add the blue hydrangea in the same manner so that the entire form is covered.
5 Cut the blue iris in approximately 5 – 6-inch lengths and insert the stems in and around the hydrangea, covering the sides and top of the wreath, letting the top petals of the iris rise slightly above the hydrangea.
6 Insert the purple lantana blossoms evenly around the wreath so that they float above the hydrangea and iris.
7 As a finishing touch, insert lengths of green ivy into the wreath form, focusing on the inside and outside edges.

Deep in the heart of the Indian Ocean in the Seychelles archipelago, Cerf Island is an exotic destination of tranquil beauty, a small island known for its remote exclusivity and private sandy beaches. Cerf is also apparently renowned for its mangoes, which are impossibly tasty and sweet – an island delicacy and tropical treat. Here, I've combined mangoes and limes in the spirit of the Seychelles and faraway island fantasies.

SEYCHELLES MANGO LIME

WHAT *you'll need*

TOOLS: Bark wire
Straight wire (heavier gauge)
Straight wire (thinner gauge)
Bullion wire
4-inch water picks

MATERIALS:
1 18-inch straw wreath form
8 mangoes
6 - 8 bags of small limes (45 count)
1 ½-inch ribbon
Sprigs of ivy

OPTIONAL
1 bunch green hypericum berries

HOW-TO *instructions*

1 Wrap the wreath with bark wire to create a loop for hanging.
2 Create the base layer of green ribbon using the ruched ribbon technique.
3 Wire a mango to the wreath using the heavier gauge straight wire, piercing through the center and tying the wire securely together in back.
4 Add all of the mangos, spacing them evenly throughout the form.
5 Using the thinner gauge straight wire, string limes together to fit around the mangoes. Wire individual limes to cover any gaps.
6 Continue adding limes until the entire surface is covered with fruit.
7 Add clippings of geranium foliage and ivy to the top of the wreath as a finishing touch.
8 For additional texture, insert small sprigs of hypericum berries in water picks and place them evenly throughout the wreath.

WHAT *you'll need*

TOOLS: Bark wire
1 roll of 1 ½ moss green ribbon
Bullion wire
Straight wire (thinner gauge)
Wire cutters
Clippers
4-inch water picks
6-inch wired wood picks

MATERIALS:
1 18-inch grapevine wreath
75 oranges
2 stems fuchsia phalaenopsis orchids
1 bunch fuchsia mokara orchids
1 bunch green hypericum berries
1 bunch red hypericum berries
1 bunch of holly

Located off the southern coast of Italy in the Mediterranean Sea, Sicily is a magical place of ancient ruins and temples, lush landscapes and varied cultural and architectural history, resulting from multiple layers of influences. In Sicily, it's possible to see relics from the Phoenicians and Greeks to the Roman, Byzantine and Norman empires – sometimes even altogether in one place! Throughout the island, inspiring art and architecture, wondrous archeological sites and unique cultural traditions mix together in a colorful, riotous harmony. Inspired by the vivid orange and fuchsia colors of ancient frescoes and landscapes, I created this wreath of oranges and orchids in celebration of Sicilian colors and symbols: blood oranges and bougainvillea – ubiquitous emblems of Sicily.

| SICILIAN ORANGES & ORCHIDS

HOW-TO *instructions*

1 Wrap the bark wire around the frame to create a loop for hanging.
2 Create a base layer of ribbon using the ruched ribbon technique.
3 String 4 oranges together on the straight wire, creating a garland.
4 Place the garland of oranges across the wreath, covering the top and sides, wrapping the wire ends around, tying them securely in the back. Clip the excess wire.
5 Working in horizontal rows, continue adding rows of oranges, wrapping and tying the wires, until the entire wreath is covered, clipping the excess wire.
6 Cut the phalaenopsis stems into individual blossoms; insert the stems into water picks and place them in and around the wreath.
7 Cut the mokara orchids into 3-inch pieces; insert the stems into water picks and place them throughout the wreath.
8 Continue the process of adding accent materials: using the wire wood picks, wire small pieces of berries and insert them into the wreath so that they float above the surface.
9 As a finishing touch, wire small pieces of holly (3-inches) using the wood picks, inserting them into the wreath, filling gaps and adding a touch of greenery throughout the wreath.

DESIGN *note*

Consider using faux orchids
for a longer-lasting wreath.

One of the most charming myths associated with the magical and beautiful Northern Lights is the Finnish saga of the "revonlulet," the arctic fire fox. Legend has it that arctic foxes created the northern lights by streaking throughout the sky, generating sparks as they brushed against rugged, snow-capped mountain peaks. As the sparks mixed with snow, illuminating the night sky, they created the aurora—resulting in ribbons of color and bands of emerald and violet light that dance each winter between the starts. Colorful and striking, this wreath of sparkling mesh and cellophane with accents of purple petunias and green peppers is designed to capture the sense of striated bright colors and pulsating light of the inspiring "fire fox" Northern Lights.

NORTHERN LIGHTS

WHAT *you'll need*

TOOLS:
Bark wire
Straight wire (thinner gauge)
Bullion wire
Clippers
Wire cutters
Scissors
6-inch wired wood picks
4-inch water picks

MATERIALS:
1 18-inch straw wreath form
1 roll of blue mesh ribbon
1 roll of green mesh ribbon
1 role of purple mesh ribbon
1 roll of turquoise cellophane
1 roll of green cellophane
10 lime green bell peppers
Purple petunias
Purple potato vine
Green trailing ivy

HOW-TO *instructions*   3 Expert   5-7 D

1 Wrap the bark wire around the wreath to create a loop for hanging.
2 Create a base layer of alternating colors of mesh ribbon using the ruched ribbon technique, covering the entire wreath form with color and texture.
3 Cut the turquoise and cellophane into 4 inch squares.
4 Pinch the cellophane in the center, wrapping the point with the bullion wire to create a floret form.
5 Using a continuous length of bullion wire, create garlands of 5 – 6 florets, leaving about 4 inches in between.
6 Create garlands of green cellophane in the same manner.
7 Wire the garlands to the wood picks and insert them in the wreath, focusing on the edges and weaving some across the form until the entire wreath is covered.
8 Using the straight wire, pierce the bell pepper in the middle and wire it to the wreath, wrap the ends to the back and twist tightly to secure. Clip excess wire.
9 Clip small cuttings of petunias, insert them in water picks and place throughout the wreath so that the blooms float above the survace.
10 Using the wood picks, wire trailing ivy and insert it throughout the wreath.
11 As a finishing touch, insert clippings of purple potato vine in water picks and add them to the wreath.

DESIGN *note*

For extra brilliance and illumination, weave in strings of LED lights in and around the layers of mesh..

Nantucket Island is situated off the Eastern seaboard of the U.S., 30 miles east of Boston, surrounded by the Atlantic Ocean, a quaint and historic place, steeped in maritime traditions. Wind-swept and rugged, the island is often obscured by rolling banks of grey fog and mist, thus lending Nantucket its unofficial nickname of "the grey lady." One of the most iconic and romantic images of Nantucket is the grey-shingled cottages that are almost completely obliterated by ethereal clouds of pink-petaled climbing roses in summer. This wreath of grey stones and pink roses is inspired by the historic architecture and lush roses and gardens of the charming island of Nantucket.

HOW-TO *instructions*

1   Cut the plastic bag into 5-inch strips and wrap evenly around the entire wreath to create a solid base layer.
2   Wrap the bark wire around the wreath to create a loop for hanging.
3   Paint the sides and top of the wreath with taupe gray paint and let it dry completely.
4   Working left to right in rows around the sides and top of the form, hot glue the gravel to cover the entire surface.
5   Cut pieces of bind wire and twist them together to form a small 3-dimensional shape, crafting enough pieces to form an outer garland.
6   Spray the forms with the gray craft paint.
7   Attach the crafted garland to the wreath, securing the wire ends at intervals to the grape vine frame.
8   Place the wreath on a metal platter or hang vertically on a door.
9   Fill the small water tubes with water and tuck them in the paper wire garland, placing them in a zig-zag pattern around the wreath.
10 Cut short stems of pink spray roses, hydrangea and waxflower and tuck them in the water tubes at varying heights, creating clusters around the wreath.

NANTUCKET ROSE

WHAT *you'll need*

TOOLS: Bark wire
         Clippers
         Wire cutters
         Paint brush
         Hot glue
         Glue gun
         Natural paper-covered bind wire
         Small water tubes

MATERIALS:
         1 18-inch grapevine wreath
         1 large plastic bag, cut into 5-inch strips
         Taupe gray paint
         Light gray craft spray paint
         10 pounds of gray gravel
         1 bunch of pink spray roses
         1 bunch of pink waxflower
         3 stems pink hyndrangea
         Large weathered tin platter
           (optional for table display)

WHAT *you'll need*

TOOLS: Bark wire
Bullion wire
Straight wire (thinner gauge)
Clippers
Wire cutters
Scissors
Hot glue
Hot glue gun
6-inch wired wood picks
4-inch water picks

MATERIALS:
1 18-inch grapevine wreath
Several sheets of plain white paper
3 bags of medium marshmallows
2 bags of plastic eggs in pastel colors
1 bag of small chocolate eggs in pastel colors
2 bunches of cream daffodils
1 bunch of yellow daffodils
1 bunch of pussy willow branches
White feathers

At Easter time, the sweet sentiments of spring – of renewal and hope, beauty and joy – are always on full display, bursting forth in gardens and in our hearts, providing inspiration. The iconic symbols of Easter – bunnies, marshmallows, hats, feathers, chocolate eggs and spring flowers in every shade of pastel hue – evoke warm feelings and gentle thoughts, uplifting our moods in tune with the season. This fanciful spring wreath of marshmallows, chocolate eggs and flowers with a bunny medallion celebrates this Easter springtime dream.

EASTER BUNNY

HOW-TO *instructions*

1 Wrap the bark wire around the wreath to create a loop for hanging.
2 Cut the white paper into 3-inch squares, gathering each piece in the center and securing it with bullion wire.
3 Working from left to right in rows around the wreath, glue the paper forms onto the frame to create the base layer.
4 Using the straight wire, pierce the marshmallows, stringing 4 together.
5 Working in rows, lay the marshmallow garlands across the wreath, wrapping the ends around to secure in the back, covering the entire wreath. Cut the excess wire.
6 Using the bullion wire, string 3 plastic eggs together, alternating the pastel colors.
7 Working in rows around the wreath, wrap the egg garlands around the form, twisting the ends together in the back.
8 Next, pierce the chocolate eggs with straight wire, stringing 4 together.
9 Wrap the chocolate egg garlands around the wreath so that they float above the base layers.
10 Insert the daffodils, cut to 3 – 4-inch lengths, in water picks and place in and around the wreath.
11 Using the bullion wire, create garlands of feathers.
12 Weave the feather garlands in and around the wreath.
13 Wire pieces of pussy willow branches to wood picks and insert at an angle in the wreath, focusing on the interior and exterior edges.
14 Add an Easter bunny medallion as a finishing touch, crafted from mini-marshmallows and papier mache.

Throughout the ages, artists have been drawn to flowers as a premier, inspiring topic. Claude Monet famously painted water lilies while Vincent Van Gogh obviously excelled in sunflowers. In the 17th century, Dutch Master painters depicted poetic still-life tableaus of fruits and flowers that offered a glimpse into European domestic life. An artist who is perhaps best known for her zinnia paintings is southern folk artist Clementine Hunter — a remarkable woman who first started painting in her 50s. Zinnias are a ubiquitous feature of the southern garden and Hunter showcased them in a unique way, highlighting their fresh charm and vibrancy, evoking a nostalgic mood. This late summer wreath of plums and zinnias makes a strong statement of simple beauty in rich plum and berry tones – inspired by Ms. Hunter's favorite flower and her compelling art.

PLUMBERRY ZINNIA

WHAT *you'll need*

TOOLS:
Bark wire
1 roll of 1 ½ inch berry ribbon
Straight wire (thinner gauge)
Bullion wire
Clippers
Scissors
Wire cutters
4-inch water picks
6-inch water picks

MATERIALS:
1 18-inch grapevine wreath
100 red plums
1 bunch of fuchsia zinnias
1 bunch red hypericum berry
Petite pink petunias
Green ivy

HOW-TO *instructions*

 2 Medium 5-7 D

1   Wrap the bark wire around the wreath form to create a loop for hanging.

2   Create a berry ribbon base layer using the ruched ribbon technique.

3   Using the straight wire, pierce the plums, stringing 4 together.

4   Lay the plum garland across the wreath, covering the sides and top.

5   Wrap the ends of the wire around the wreath, tying them securely in back. Clip the excess wire.

6   Working in rows continue adding the plum string in this manner until the entire wreath is covered.

7   Cut the zinnias to 3 – 4 inches, insert in water picks and place them around the wreath to achieve an aesthetic presentation.

8   Cut the hypericum berries and petunias in similar small pieces, insert in water picks and add them to the wreath, focusing on the interior and outside edges.

9   As a finishing touch, add trailing ivy as a light border.

In the ethereal poem "Autumn Fires" by Robert Louis Stevenson, the transition between summer and fall is described as an allegory of beauty and passage of time. His eloquent prose: "Sing a song of Seasons! Something bright in all! Flowers in the summer, fires in the fall" highlights the changing landscape as August fades away and September holds court – when summer's bounty lingers on as vibrant colors fade and gently mellow, and then crystallizes into brilliant, blazing hues. This wreath of summer citrus fruit and flowers celebrates a magical midsummer night's dream right before the first frost and advent of fall.

MIDSUMMER NIGHT'S DREAM

WHAT *you'll need*

TOOLS:
Bark wire
1 roll of 1 ½ inch orange ribbon
Straight wire (thinner gauge)
Bullion wire
Clippers
Scissors
Wire cutters
4-inch water picks
6-inch wired wood picks

MATERIALS:
1 18-inch grapevine wreath
8 bags of tangerines (approximately 80 count)
3 bags of purple pearl onions
1 bunch of fuchsia zinnia
1 bunch of burgundy zinnia
1 bunch orange alstromeria
Green trailing ivy

HOW-TO *instructions*

(2 Medium)   (5-7 D)

1 Wrap the bark wire around the wreath form to create a loop for hanging.
2 Create an orange ribbon base layer using the ruched ribbon technique.
3 Working side to side across the top of the wreath, attach the ruched ribbon garland to cover the top and sides of the wreath.
4 Using the straight wire, pierce the tangerines, stringing 4 together.
5 Lay the tangerine garland across the wreath, covering the sides and top.
6 Wrap the end of the wire around the wreath, tying them securely in back. Clip the excess wire.
7 Working in rows, continue adding individual strings of tangerines in this manner until the entire wreath is covered.
8 Using the straight wire, string 4 -5 pearl onions together, wrap the ends around and secure in the back.
9 Lay the pearl onion garlands over the top of the tangerines so that they float a bit above the surface, wrapping and securing the wires in the same manner until the wreath is covered.
10 Cut the flowers into small 3 – 4 inch pieces and insert in the water picks, placing them in and around the wreath.
11 As a finishing touch, add sprigs of ivy, focusing on the interior and outside edges.

WHAT *you'll need*

TOOLS:
: Bark wire
  Clippers
  Wire cutters
  Scissors
  6-inch wired wood picks

MATERIALS:
: 1 21-inch floral foam wreath
  1 skein lavender wool
  1 skein pale turquoise wool
  1 bunch (25) grey knight rose
  1 bunch (25) early grey rose
  1 bag cream reindeer moss
  1 bunch cream hydrangea (fresh or dried)
  1 bunch lavender hydrangea
  1 bunch lavender mokara orchids
  1 roll of red and white stripe ribbon
  1 roll of pale gold ribbon

A little known exhibit in the heart of Paris is the *Musee des Arts Forain*, the museum of fairground arts located in the *Pavillons de Bercy* in the 12th arrondisement. Off the beaten tourist path and accessible by appointment only, the museum is a hidden gem in the City of Light. Although it requires more than the usual thought and planning with advance reservations required, a visit is well worth the effort: the museum is a magical place of endless inspiration, featuring whimsical puppet theaters and Venetian-themed carousel rides, a collection of unique and mesmerizing displays. The vintage Parisian carousel of muted colors and fanciful forms, worn by weather and time, is especially compelling, attracting children and adults alike with a merry-go-round of prancing and dancing carved wooden horses that twirl across a gaily painted platform. This wreath of vintage roses and summer flowers with fanciful candy stripe ribbon trim is designed to evoke the magical joie de vivre of a vintage carousel ride, enhanced by the splendid backdrop of Paris.

| VINTAGE CAROUSEL

HOW-TO *instructions*

1 Wrap the bark wire around the wreath, doubling it, to create a loop for hanging.
2 Soak the wreath in water until it is completely saturated.
3 Using the wood picks, wire the reindeer moss in small bundles and insert onto the wreath form to create a base layer.
4 Cut the roses to 4 – 5-inch lengths and insert them around the wreath, angling them to create a sense of movement, extending placement above the form.
5 Add small pieces of hydrangea in and around the wreath, filling in the space around the roses.
6 Cut the orchids into 4-inch lengths and insert in the wreath so that the blooms float slightly above the other materials.
7 Cut the wool into 4-inch pieces, wiring the middle to the wood pick, and insert in the wreath for texture.
8 Cut the red and gold ribbons into 10-inch lengths, pinching the middle and wiring them to wood picks, creating a banner effect.
9 Insert the ribbons around the edge of the wreath as a finishing touch.

WHAT *you'll need*

TOOLS: Bark wire & bullion wire in several colors
Hot glue & hot glue gun
Clippers
Wire cutters + scissors
6-inch wired wood picks
4-inch water picks

MATERIALS:
1 18-inch square grapevine wreath
2 bunches fresh (or preserved) eucalyptus
1 roll of blue + green cellophane
2 bunches of green aspidistra
2 bunches of variegated aspidistra
1 bunch lemon leaf salal
Colored beads
Colored wood popsicle sticks
Feather butterflies (from the craft store)
1 bunch of salmon zinnias
1 bunch of fuchsia zinnias
Pink lantana
Peach and purple petunias

Every year when I travel to Paris, I gravitate to the Tuileries and Luxembourg Gardens, the beautiful and iconic gardens in the center of the city that are always an incredible source of seasonal inspiration. In the fall, colorful mums spill over stone urns in lush cascades, while the winter season highlights evergreen topiaries and hardy blooms that are planted with precision in classical patterns and motifs. By the spring and summer, the flowers take center stage – dominating the space with lush plantings and colorful blooms that attract birds and butterflies, creating a magical effect. Sitting in a quiet glade, it's possible to see a kaleidoscope of butterflies flitting from one flower to the next, evoking a sense of joy and wonder in an inspiring Parisian garden dream scene. This wreath of stylized butterflies, made of folded green leaves and colored beads, floats in and around a bed of summer flowers, including zinnias, petunias and lantana – hinting at the Parisian garden party-themed fête inside.

| SPRINGTIME IN PARIS

HOW-TO *instructions*

3 Expert   5-7 D

1   Wrap the bark wire around the wreath to create a loop for hanging.
2   Cut the eucalyptus into small pieces, bundling 3 – 4 together with the bullion wire.
3   Working side to side in rows, insert the bundles into the grapevine frame until the sides and top are completely covered, creating the base layer.
4   Cut the cellophane into 4-inch squares, pinch in the middle and tie with the bullion wire.
5   Tuck the cellophane into the eucalyptus, scattering it evenly throughout the wreath for additional texture.
6   Using the leaf-folding technique, create upper butterfly wings with the aspidistra. Glue lemon leaves together to create the lower wings.
7   Glue the leaves to the underside of the wood stick, creating the butterfly.
8   Finish the butterflies by gluing colored beads to the stick and on the wings.
9   Create 12 – 15 butterflies.
10 Wire the butterflies to the wood picks and insert in the form, covering the entire wreath, attaching them to float at various levels.
11 Insert the feather butterflies in and around the wreath.
12 As a finishing touch, add the zinnias, petunias and lantana, inserting them in water picks and then into the wreath.

When I saw Yayoi Kusuma's blockbuster museum exhibit of "Infinity Rooms" featuring brightly colored works displayed in her signature mirror-lined walls, I was intrigued by the use of pattern and repetition, especially her long-standing obsession with polka dots -- a metaphor for infinity – which she says she sees everywhere. The exhibit was powerful and inspiring, but what was most memorable were the words of the artist herself, conveyed in a compelling monologue that played continuously on a screen. Kusama said that she produces art in the hope we will understand her vision and dream; she wants people to be inspired for the "benefit of world peace and love." This wreath of polka dot apples celebrates Kusama's favorite motif as well as her indomitable artistic spirit.

POLKA DOT APPLES

WHAT *you'll need*

TOOLS: Bark wire
Bullion wire
Straight wire (thinner gauge)
Small scoop
6-inch wired wood picks
4-inch water picks
Tooth picks

MATERIALS:
1 18-inch grapevine wreath
1 roll of 1 ½-inch green ribbon
3 bags of golden apples (27 total)
3 bags of green apples (27 total)
2 pounds of small green apples
  (or small green peppers)
1 bunch of green hypericum berries
2 bunches of yellow craspedia (billy balls)
Sprigs of yellow begonia blossoms
Green ivy

HOW-TO *instructions*

1 Wrap the bark wire around the wreath to create a loop for hanging.
2 Craft a ribbon base layer using the ruched ribbon technique.
3 Using the straight wire, pierce the apples, stringing 3 together, alternating the yellow and green colors.
4 Lay the apple garlands across the wreath, wrap the wire ends around and twist together in back. Cut the excess wire.
5 Working in rows, continue adding yellow and green apple garlands in this manner until the entire wreath is covered.
6 Using the small scoop, carve polka dots in the apples, replacing the green dot with the yellow piece and vice vers, attaching the polka dot apple pieces with tooth picks.
7 Continue adding polka dots in this manner until the entire wreath is covered.
8 Attach the small apples or peppers to the wood picks and insert them evenly around the wreath.
9 Add the craspedia using the wood picks, interspersing them.
10 Insert sprigs of hypericum berry and begonia in water tubes and place them to float slightly above the fruit.
11 As a finishing touch, add the ivy using wood picks, focusing on the interior and outer edges.

In the timeless and enchanting Tchaikovsky ballet the "Nutcracker Suite," a young girl becomes besotted with a carved wooden nutcracker that magically transforms into a handsome prince. In her dreams, the prince leads her through a moonlit forest where snowflakes dance and then on to a beautiful Land of Sweets where a Sugar Plum Fairy reigns. Taking inspiration from this iconic Christmas classic, this giant oversized wreath of twinkling lights, vintage glass ornaments, tulle fabric, winter birds, fanciful butterflies and glistening crystal branches in an ethereal, wintry palette of ice pink, pale lilac, and plum – is designed to conjure the magic of the holiday spirit – and the sweet dreams of Christmas.

| SWEET DREAMS

WHAT *you'll need*

TOOLS: Bark wire and cording
4 spools green paddle wire
Straight wire (thinner gauge)
2 spools gold bullion wire
Clippers, wire cutters, scissors
6-inch wired wood picks

MATERIALS:
1 6 ft. faux evergreen wreath
2 faux evergreen garlands
6 boxes of pink LED lights
8 pink + 5 lilac organza sheets
3 purple/plum/gold ornament balls
3 small purple/plum/gold ornament balls
3 silver glitter fern branches
25 lbs. of fingerling potatoes
2 can gold spray paint (for potatoes)
5 purple spray ornaments
2 rolls of purple 2-inch ribbon
2 bunches purple glitter branches
2 bunches pink tulle ribbon
1 fuchsia 2-inch ribbon
30 paper rosettes (in various sizes)
20 small gift-wrapped boxes

HOW-TO *instructions*

1 Wrap the bark wire around the wreath to create a loop for hanging.
2 Using the bind wire, attach the 2 faux garlands to the top of the wreath form.
3 Wrap the pink and lavender organza loosely around the wreath.
4 String the lights onto the wreath, weaving them in and around the organza, leaving a length of cord at the end for plugging in.
5 Begin adding the ornaments and potatoes, wiring them to the bullion wire in rows across the wreath, stringing several together, tying the wire ends together in back.
6 Place the gift-wrapped boxes in coordinating colored ribbons and papers so that they are evenly distributed throughout, wiring them to the form.
7 Attach the paper rosettes, placing them around the ornaments and gift boxes.
8 Continue adding layers of small ornaments, creating garlands with the bullion wire, wiring them so that they float above the wreath.
9 Create 5-inch lengths of ruched purple ribbon, wire them to the wood picks and insert them in the wreath, including the inside and outside edges.
10 Using the ruched ribbon technique, create tulle and glitter branch garlands, attaching them to the interior and outside edges.
11 Cut the silver ferns into small pieces, wire to the wood picks, and insert.
12 Hang the wreath using the strong cording; wrap ruched ribbon tulle around it.
13 Plug the LED lights into an electrical outlet to illuminate the wreath.

Across the sprawling savannah of the Serengeti National Park in northeastern Tanzania, day-break arrives as a glint on the horizon, just as it has done since the dawn of time, replacing the darkness with a soft orange glow. All of a sudden, just as the sunlight expands and unfolds in bands of peach and bronze, the spell-binding scene is enhanced by movement and sound as slumbering wildlife come to life, creating a vivid dream of wild, untamed beauty. Inspired by these colors and textures of the African landscape, this wreath captures the magical feeling of a Serengeti sunrise with tiger stripe lilies, amber-scented trumpet vine and bold orange fruits.

SERENGETI SUNRISE

WHAT *you'll need*

TOOLS: Bark wire
Gold bullion wire
Straight wire (thinner gauge)
6-inch wired wood picks
4-inch water picks

MATERIALS:
1 18-inch grapevine wreath
1 roll of 3-inch burlap/linen ribbon
1 roll of 3-inch bronze/brown ribbon
1 roll of 1 ½-inch orange ribbon
60 apricots
1 pound of orange habanero peppers
1 bunch bronze kangaroo paw
10 stems of orange day lily
1 bunch of orange trumpet vine

DESIGN *note*

Use the wired wood picks to insert additional apricots to fill in gaps if needed.

HOW-TO *instructions*   3 Expert   5-7 D

1 Wrap the bark wire around the wreath to create a loop for hanging.
2 Using the burlap ribbon, create a base layer with the ruched ribbon technique.
3 Pierce the apricots close to the center with the straight wire, stringing 3 together.
4 Lay the apricot garland across the top of the wreath, wrapping ends around to the back, twisting the wire to secure. Cut the excess wire.
5 Working in even rows around the wreath, continue adding the apricots in this manner until the entire wreath is covered.
6 Next, create pepper garlands, stringing 2 together.
7 Working in rows, add the pepper garlands, spacing them evenly around the wreath, twisting the ends to secure.
8 Using the bullion wire, create garlands of kangaroo paw, wiring short pieces together, leaving a few inches of space in between.
9 Lay the kangaroo paw garlands across the wreath so that they float above the fruit. Tie the bullion wire to the straight wire to secure.
10 Insert the day lilies in water picks and place throughout the wreath.
11 Using longer lengths of trumpet vine in water picks, insert the vines and blossoms around the wreath, focusing on the interior and outside edges. Leave some of the foliage on the vine.

In 1956, French filmmaker Albert Lamorisse made an enchanting short film about a little boy and his red balloon. Part children's story, part timeless essay on the power of love, the film chronicles the tale of a child's special relationship with a red balloon as they encounter various obstacles throughout the streets of Paris. When a mob of classmates stalk the boy in an effort to destroy the balloon – and ultimately succeed – we feel the boy's sadness and grief as he sits with the shriveled balloon, mourning the loss of his cherished friend. But just as the last gasp of helium escapes from the red balloon, the boy is suddenly surrounded by every balloon in Paris that has magically gathered around him, creating a powerful statement of camaraderie and support. In the final scene, the balloons lift the boy high above Paris, where he floats off into the sunset. This floating wreath of red balloons, accented with red pears, apples and cherry tomatoes, is designed to capture the key themes of this lovely film: the power of hope and love and the invincible strength of the human spirit.

HOW-TO *instructions*

1 Wrap the bark wire around the wreath to create a loop for hanging.
2 Next, wrap the fuchsia ribbon around the wreath, covering the entire surface to create the base layer.
3 Using the straight wire, pierce the red apples, stringing 2 together.
4 Lay the apple garland across the wreath, wrap ends around to the back and twist together tightly in back. Clip the excess wire.
5 Continue adding apple garlands, spacing them evenly around the wreath.
6 Add the pears in the same manner, spreading the garlands evenly.
7 Blow up the balloons to about 3 – 4-inches in size. Knot the ends.
8 Create garlands of 4 balloons with the bullion wire, leaving 3-inches in between.
9 Working in rows around the wreath, place the balloon garlands, wrapping the wire ends around and twist together, position the balloons around the fruit.
10 Cut the cellophane into 4-inch squares, pinch the middle and wrap with the bullion wire to create a stylized floret.
11 Make a cellophane border by creating several garlands of 5 pointed florets with the bullion wire, attaching one end of the garland to the wood pick.
12 Insert the wood pick into the side of the wreath and weave the cellophane florets around the edge.
13 Continue adding the cellophane garlands until the entire wreath is surrounded.
14 As a finishing touch, tuck clippings of petunias (or other small fuchsia-colored flowers) into the wreath, using the water picks.

| LE BALLON ROUGE

WHAT *you'll need*

TOOLS: Bark wire
Straight wire (thinner gauge)
Bullion wire
Clippers
Wire cutters
Scissors
6-inch wired wood picks
4-inch water picks

MATERIALS:
1 18-inch straw wreath
1 roll of 3-inch fuchsia ribbon
1 roll of fuchsia cellophane
10 bags of red balloons
  (12-inch x 15 pieces) = 150
2 bags of small red apples
2 bags of small red pears
2 pints of red cherry tomatoes
Fuchsia petunia blossoms

| "A Gift of Gratitude"

This book on wreaths was pure joy to conceptualize, create and produce -- the natural progression of my first two books on "Floral Diplomacy" and "A White House Christmas" that focused on my White House experience as the venue for my floral work. In the Christmas book, I share some of my favorite White House projects and how to create them, including a few wreaths – a precursor of this book and the launch of my new floral design series.

As I've travelled around the country over the past two years, leading floral design workshops and conducting book signings, the experience has left a strong impression. Without a doubt, engaging in conversation with like-minded people who are passionate about flowers and design is absolutely the best part of my job. While audiences are naturally interested in White House anecdotes and behind-the-scenes stories, I've noticed that the conversation quickly turns to "how-to" topics – specific questions about floral techniques, inspiration and design.

For many years, my dream has been to write a floral design book – a technical handbook with tips and tricks interspersed with inspirational images and text about the creative process, the kind of book that I would include in my own reference library. Inspired by feedback from my book tour audiences and social media followers – who seem especially intrigued by my wreath designs – my new series of floral art books launches with wreaths, to be followed by a full range of floral art themes and ideas.

Once again, I am grateful for my brilliant team at Stichting Kunstboek – Publisher Karel Puype, Editor Katrien Van Moerbeke and designer Jan de Coster for their talent and expertise. Each time we work together, they help me visualize an exciting concept woven together by text and images, presented in engaging, elegant formats with sophisticated graphic design. I am also impressed by their professionalism and efficiency; they've made the process of writing 3 books in 2 ½ years such a (relatively) easy, breezy pursuit that is always a pleasure!

Photography is the essential element for any design book and is even more important when it comes to "how-to" manuals. For the 12 years, I've been fortunate to work with Kevin Allen, who always portrays my flowers and wreaths with such precision and sensitivity – perfectly capturing my vision and intent. He took the bulk of the wreath photos in this book. In addition, it's been a pleasure working with Sunni Kim Cook on this project, who has a fantastic eye for composition and detail – and the ability to create images with a uniquely fresh, modern feeling. Sunni is responsible for the "how-to" photos as well as a few wreath shots, too. I am also grateful for the artistry of Georgianna Lane, whose evocative and ethereal shots are always swoon-worthy. I appreciate the contributions of the brilliant Erik Kvalsik and talented Dominik Ketz as well as the photography of Louise Krafft, who took the orange peel wreath image – a sentimental favorite.

I am so appreciative of the generosity of my friends and neighbors in Old Town Alexandria, who graciously lend me their doors throughout the year as a backdrop for my creations. I've surprised more than a few of their family members who are always startled to see me standing right outside their door, clippers and wires in hand. With its historic architecture and quaint traditions, Old Town is the perfect setting for portraying the possibilities of wreaths.

Writing a book can be an all-consuming project that requires a village of support. A big bouquet of gratitude is therefore in order for all of my friends and family members who enthusiastically helped with every phase of the project from brain-storming wreath concepts and photo-styling to copy edits, publicity and recipe reviews, especially Lola Honeybone, Gudrun Cottenier, Ashley Greer and Evelyn Alemanni. As always, my husband, Bob Weinhagen, is a patient and supportive presence behind-the-scenes; I appreciate his witty repartee, encouragement and love.

Finally, I am grateful to you, the reader, for joining me on this creative journey with wreaths. My sincere wish is that you find inspiration in this art of creative expression that leads to beauty – in your home, in your community and, thanks to social media, can float like the red balloon to reach a broad, international audience, inspiring others along the way.

Author
Laura Dowling
www.lauradowling.com

Layout
www.groupvandamme.eu

Published by
Stichting Kunstboek bvba
Legeweg 165
B-8020 Oostkamp
info@stichtingkunstboek.com
www.stichtingkunstboek.com

ISBN 978-90-5856-603-4
D/2018/6407/16
NUR 421

Printed in the EU

Previously published

Laura Dowling
FLORAL DIPLOMACY
at the White House
ISBN 978-90-5856-558-7

Laura Dowling
A WHITE HOUSE CHRISTMAS
Including floral design tutorials
ISBN 978-90-5856-575-4